Dramatic Idyls by Robert Browning

Series I & II

Robert Browning is one of the most significant Victorian Poets and, of course, English Poetry.

Much of his reputation is based upon his mastery of the dramatic monologue although his talents encompassed verse plays and even a well-regarded essay on Shelley during a long and prolific career.

He was born on May 7th, 1812 in Walmouth, London. Much of his education was home based and Browning was an eclectic and studious student, learning several languages and much else across a myriad of subjects, interests and passions.

Browning's early career began promisingly. The fragment from his intended long poem Pauline brought him to the attention of Dante Gabriel Rossetti, and was followed by Paracelsus, which was praised by both William Wordsworth and Charles Dickens. In 1840 the difficult Sordello, which was seen as willfully obscure, brought his career almost to a standstill.

Despite these artistic and professional difficulties his personal life was about to become immensely fulfilling. He began a relationship with, and then married, the older and better known Elizabeth Barrett. This new foundation served to energise his writings, his life and his career.

During their time in Italy they both wrote much of their best work. With her untimely death in 1861 he returned to London and thereafter began several further major projects.

The collection Dramatis Personae (1864) and the book-length epic poem The Ring and the Book (1868-69) were published and well received; his reputation as a venerated English poet now assured.

Robert Browning died in Venice on December 12th, 1889.

Index of Contents

FIRST SERIES

The Dramatic Idyls, a group of poems which indicated a return to Browning's earlier manner, furnished the title for two successive volumes, the first series published in 1879, the second the year following. The poems in the first series were composed while Browning and his sister were sojourning in a mountain hotel near the summit of the Splügen Pass in the summer of 1878. So stimulated was Browning by the mountain air that he composed with extraordinary rapidity, even for him, bringing down upon himself his sister's determined caution.

MARTIN RELPH

My grandfather says he remembers he saw, when a youngster long ago,
On a bright May day, a strange old man, with a beard as white as snow,
Stand on the hill outside our town like a monument of woe,
And, striking his bare bald head the while, sob out the reason—so!

If I last as long as Methuselah I shall never forgive myself:
But—God forgive me, that I pray, unhappy Martin Relph,
As coward, coward I call him—him, yes, him! Away from me!
Get you behind the man I am now, you man that I used to be!

What can have sewed my mouth up, set me a-stare, all eyes, no tongue?
People have urged, "You visit a scare too hard on a lad so young!
You were taken aback, poor boy," they urge, "no time to regain your wits:
Besides it had maybe cost your life." Ay, there is the cap which fits!

So, cap me, the coward,—thus! No fear! A cuff on the brow does good:
The feel of it hinders a worm inside which bores at the brain for food.
See now, there certainly seems excuse: for a moment, I trust, dear friends,
The fault was but folly, no fault of mine, or if mine, I have made amends!

For, every day that is first of May, on the hill-top, here stand I,
Martin Relph, and I strike my brow, and publish the reason why,
When there gathers a crowd to mock the fool. No fool, friends, since the bite
Of a worm inside is worse to bear: pray God I have balked him quite!

I 'll tell you. Certainly much excuse! It came of the way they cooped

Us peasantry up in a ring just here, close huddling because tight-hooped
By the red-coats round us villagers all: they meant we should see the sight
And take the example,—see, not speak, for speech was the Captain's right.

"You clowns on the slope, beware!" cried he: "This woman about to die
Gives by her fate fair warning to such acquaintance as play the spy.
Henceforth who meddle with matters of state above them perhaps will learn
That peasants should stick to their ploughtail, leave to the King the King's concern.

"Here 's a quarrel that sets the land on fire, between King George and his foes:
What call has a man of your kind—much less, a woman—to interpose?
Yet you needs must be meddling, folk like you, not foes—so much the worse!
The many and loyal should keep themselves unmixed with the few perverse.

"Is the counsel hard to follow? I gave it you plainly a month ago,
And where was the good? The rebels have learned just all that they need to know.
Not a month since in we quietly marched: a week, and they had the news,
From a list complete of our rank and file to a note of our caps and shoes.

"All about all we did and all we were doing and like to do!
Only, I catch a letter by luck, and capture who wrote it, too.
Some of you men look black enough, but the milk-white face demure
Betokens the finger foul with ink: 't is a woman who writes, be sure!

"Is it 'Dearie, how much I miss your mouth!'—good natural stuff, she pens?
Some sprinkle of that, for a blind, of course: with talk about cocks and hens,
How 'robin has built on the apple-tree, and our creeper which came to grief
Through the frost, we feared, is twining afresh round casement in famous leaf.'

"But all for a blind! She soon glides frank into 'Horrid the place is grown
With Officers here and Privates there, no nook we may call our own:
And Farmer Giles has a tribe to house, and lodging will be to seek
For the second Company sure to come ('t is whispered) on Monday week.'

'And so to the end of the chapter! There! The murder, you see, was out:
Easy to guess how the change of mind in the rebels was brought about!
Safe in the trap would they now lie snug, had treachery made no sign:
But treachery meets a just reward, no matter if fools malign!

"That traitors had played us false, was proved—sent news which fell so pat:
And the murder was out—this letter of love, the sender of this sent that!
'T is an ugly job, though, all the same—a hateful, to have to deal
With a case of the kind, when a woman 's in fault: we soldiers need nerves of steel!

"So, I gave her a chance, despatched post-haste a message to Vincent Parkes
Whom she wrote to; easy to find he was, since one of the King's own clerks,
Ay, kept by the King's own gold in the town close by where the rebels camp:
A sort of a lawyer, just the man to betray our sort—the scamp!

"'If her writing is simple and honest and only the lover-like stuff it looks,
And if you yourself are a loyalist, nor down in the rebels' books,
Come quick,' said I, 'and in person prove you are each of you clear of crime,
Or martial law must take its course: this day next week 's the time!'

"Next week is now: does he come? Not he! Clean gone, our clerk, in a trice!
He has left his sweetheart here in the lurch: no need of a warning twice!
His own neck free, but his partner's fast in the noose still, here she stands
To pay for her fault. 'T is an ugly job: but soldiers obey commands.

"And hearken wherefore I make a speech! Should any acquaintance share
The folly that led to the fault that is now to be punished, let fools beware!
Look black, if you please, but keep hands white: and, above all else, keep wives—
Or sweethearts or what they may be—from ink! Not a word now, on your lives!"

Black? but the Pit's own pitch was white to the Captain's face—the brute
With the bloated cheeks and the bulgy nose and the bloodshot eyes to suit!
He was muddled with wine, they say: more like, he was out of his wits with fear;
He had but a handful of men, that 's true,—a riot might cost him dear.

And all that time stood Rosamund Page, with pinioned arms and face
Bandaged about, on the turf marked out for the party's firing-place.
I hope she was wholly with God: I hope 't was his angel stretched a hand
To steady her so, like the shape of stone you see in our church-aisle stand.

I hope there was no vain fancy pierced the bandage to vex her eyes,
No face within which she missed without, no questions and no replies—
"Why did you leave me to die?"—"Because" ... Oh, fiends, too soon you grin
At merely a moment of hell, like that—such heaven as hell ended in!

Let mine end too! He gave the word, up went the guns in a line.
Those heaped on the hill were blind as dumb,—for, of all eyes, only mine
Looked over the heads of the foremost rank. Some fell on their knees in prayer,
Some sank to the earth, but all shut eyes, with a sole exception there.

That was myself, who had stolen up last, had sidled behind the group:
I am highest of all on the hill-top, there stand fixed while the others stoop!
From head to foot in a serpent's twine am I tightened: I touch ground?
No more than a gibbet's rigid corpse which the fetters rust around!

Can I speak, can I breathe, can I burst—aught else but see, see, only see?
And see I do—for there comes in sight—a man, it sure must be!—
Who staggeringly, stumblingly rises, falls, rises, at random flings his weight
On and on, anyhow onward—a man that's mad he arrives too late!

Else why does he wave a something white high-flourished above his head?
Why does not he call, cry,—curse the fool!—why throw up his arms instead?

O take this fist in your own face, fool! Why does not yourself shout "Stay!
Here's a man comes rushing, might and main, with something he 's mad to say"?

And a minute, only a moment, to have hell-fire boil up in your brain,
And ere you can judge things right, choose heaven,—time 's over, repentance vain!
They level: a volley, a smoke and the clearing of smoke: I see no more
Of the man smoke hid, nor his frantic arms, nor the something white he bore.

But stretched on the field, some half-mile off, is an object. Surely dumb,
Deaf, blind were we struck, that nobody heard, not one of us saw him come!
Has he fainted through fright? One may well believe! What is it he holds so fast?
Turn him over, examine the face! Heyday! What, Vincent Parkes at last?

Dead! dead as she, by the selfsame shot: one bullet has ended both,
Her in the body and him in the soul. They laugh at our plighted troth.
"Till death us do part?" Till death us do join past parting—that sounds like
Betrothal indeed! O Vincent Parkes, what need has my fist to strike?

I helped you: thus were you dead and wed: one bound, and your soul reached hers!
There is clenched in your hand the thing, signed, sealed, the paper which plain avers
She is innocent, innocent, plain as print, with the King's Arms broad engraved:
No one can hear, but if any one high on the hill can see, she 's saved!

And torn his garb and bloody his lips with heart-break—plain it grew
How the week's delay had been brought about: each guess at the end proved true.
It was hard to get at the folk in power: such waste of time! And then
Such pleading and praying, with, all the while, his lamb in the lions' den!

And at length when he wrung their pardon out, no end to the stupid forms—
The license and leave: I make no doubt—what wonder if passion warms
The pulse in a man if you play with his heart?—he was something hasty in speech;
Anyhow, none would quicken the work: he had to beseech, beseech!

And the thing once signed, sealed, safe in his grasp,—what followed but fresh delays?
For the floods were out, he was forced to take such a roundabout of ways!
And 't was "Halt there!" at every turn of the road, since he had to cross the thick
Of the redcoats: what did they care for him and his "Quick, for God's sake, quick!"

Horse? but he had one: had it how long? till the first knave smirked "You brag
Yourself a friend of the King's? then lend to a King's friend here your nag!"
Money to buy another? Why, piece by piece they plundered him still,
With their "Wait you must,—no help: if aught can help you, a guinea will!"

And a borough there was—I forget the name—whose Mayor must have the bench
Of Justices ranged to clear a doubt: for "Vincent," thinks he, sounds French!
It well may have driven him daft, God knows! all man can certainly know
Is—rushing and falling and rising, at last he arrived in a horror—so!

When a word, cry, gasp, would have rescued both! Ay, bite me! The worm begins
At his work once more. Had cowardice proved—that only—my sin of sins!
Friends, look you here! Suppose ... suppose ... But mad I am, needs must be!
Judas the Damned would never have dared such a sin as I dream! For, see!

Suppose I had sneakingly loved her myself, my wretched self, and dreamed
In the heart of me "She were better dead than happy and his!"—while gleamed
A light from hell as I spied the pair in a perfectest embrace,
He the savior and she the saved,—bliss born of the very murder-place!

No! Say I was scared, friends! Call me fool and coward, but nothing worse!
Jeer at the fool and gibe at the coward! 'T was ever the coward's curse
That fear breeds fancies in such: such takes their shadow for substance still,
—A fiend at their back. I liked poor Parkes,—loved Vincent, if you will!

And her—why, I said "Good morrow" to her, "Good even," and nothing more:
The neighborly way! She was just to me as fifty had been before.
So, coward it is and coward shall be! There's a friend, now! Thanks! A drink
Of water I wanted: and now I can walk, get home by myself, I think.

PHEIDIPPIDES

Χαίρετε, νικῶμεν.

First I salute this soil of the blessed, river and rock!
Gods of my birthplace, dæmons and heroes, honor to all!
Then I name thee, claim thee for our patron, co-equal in praise
—Ay, with Zeus the Defender, with Her of the ægis and spear!
Also, ye of the bow and the buskin, praised be, your peer.
Now, henceforth and forever,—O latest to whom I upraise
Hand and heart and voice! For Athens, leave pasture and flock!
Present to help, potent to save, Pan—patron I call!

Archons of Athens, topped by the tettix, see, I return!
See, 'tis myself here standing alive, no spectre that speaks!
Crowned with the myrtle, did you command me, Athens and you,
"Run, Pheidippides, run and race, reach Sparta for aid!
Persia has come, we are here, where is She?" Your command I obeyed,
Ran and raced: like stubble, some field which a fire runs through,
Was the space between city and city: two days, two nights did I burn
Over the hills, under the dales, down pits and up peaks.

Into their midst I broke: breath served but for "Persia has come!
Persia bids Athens proffer slaves'-tribute, water and earth;
Razed to the ground is Eretria—but Athens, shall Athens sink,
Drop into dust and die—the flower of Hellas utterly die,

Die, with the wide world spitting at Sparta, the stupid, the stander-by?
Answer me quick, what help, what hand do you stretch o'er destruction's brink?
How,—when? No care for my limbs!—there's lightning in all and some—
Fresh and fit your message to bear, once lips give it birth!"

O my Athens—Sparta love thee? Did Sparta respond?
Every face of her leered in a furrow of envy, mistrust,
Malice,—each eye of her gave me its glitter of gratified hate!
Gravely they turned to take counsel, to cast for excuses. I stood
Quivering,—the limbs of me fretting as fire frets, an inch from dry wood:
"Persia has come, Athens asks aid, and still they debate?
Thunder, thou Zeus! Athene, are Spartans a quarry beyond
Swing of thy spear? Phoibos and Artemis, clang them 'Ye must'!"

No bolt launched from Olumpos! Lo, their answer at last!
"Has Persia come,—does Athens ask aid,—may Sparta befriend?
Nowise precipitate judgment—too weighty the issue at stake!
Count we no time lost time which lags through respect to the gods!
Ponder that precept of old, 'No warfare, whatever the odds
In your favor, so long as the moon, half-orbed, is unable to take
Full-circle her state in the sky!' Already she rounds to it fast:
Athens must wait, patient as we—who judgment suspend."

Athens,—except for that sparkle,—thy name, I had mouldered to ash!
That sent a blaze through my blood; off, off and away was I back,
—Not one word to waste, one look to lose on the false and the vile!
Yet "O gods of my land!" I cried, as each hillock and plain,
Wood and stream, I knew, I named, rushing past them again,
"Have ye kept faith, proved mindful of honors we paid you erewhile?
Vain was the filleted victim, the fulsome libation! Too rash
Love in its choice, paid you so largely service so slack!

"Oak and olive and bay,—I bid you cease to enwreathe
Brows made bold by your leaf! Fade at the Persian's foot,
You that, our patrons were pledged, should never adorn a slave!
Rather I hail thee, Parnes,—trust to thy wild waste tract!
Treeless, herbless, lifeless mountain! What matter if slacked
My speed may hardly be, for homage to crag and to cave
No deity deigns to drape with verdure? at least I can breathe,
Fear in thee no fraud from the blind, no lie from the mute!"

Such my cry as, rapid, I ran over Parnes' ridge;
Gully and gap I clambered and cleared till, sudden, a bar
Jutted, a stoppage of stone against me, blocking the way.
Right! for I minded the hollow to traverse, the fissure across:
"Where I could enter, there I depart by! Night in the fosse?
Athens to aid? Though the dive were through Erebos, thus I obey—
Out of the day dive, into the day as bravely arise! No bridge

Better!"—when—ha! what was it I came on, of wonders that are?

There, in the cool of a cleft, sat he—majestical Pan!
Ivy drooped wanton, kissed his head, moss cushioned his hoof:
All the great god was good in the eyes grave-kindly—the curl
Carved on the bearded cheek, amused at a mortal's awe,
As, under the human trunk, the goat-thighs grand I saw.
"Halt, Pheidippides!"—halt I did, my brain of a whirl:
"Hither to me! Why pale in my presence?" he gracious began:
"How is it,—Athens, only in Hellas, holds me aloof?

"Athens, she only, rears me no fane, makes me no feast!
Wherefore? Than I what godship to Athens more helpful of old?
Ay, and still, and forever her friend! Test Pan, trust me!
Go, bid Athens take heart, laugh Persia to scorn, have faith
In the temples and tombs! Go, say to Athens, 'The Goat-God saith:
When Persia—so much as strews not the soil—is cast in the sea,
Then praise Pan who fought in the ranks with your most and least,
Goat-thigh to greaved-thigh, made one cause with the free and the bold!'

"Say Pan saith: 'Let this, foreshowing the place, be the pledge!'"
(Gay, the liberal hand held out this herbage I bear
—Fennel—I grasped it a-tremble with dew—whatever it bode)
"While, as for thee" ... But enough! He was gone. If I ran hitherto—
Be sure that, the rest of my journey, I ran no longer, but flew.
Parnes to Athens—earth no more, the air was my road:
Here am I back. Praise Pan, we stand no more on the razor's edge!
Pan for Athens, Pan for me! I too have a guerdon rare!

Then spoke Miltiades. "And thee, best runner of Greece,
Whose limbs did duty indeed,—what gift is promised thyself?
Tell it us straightway,—Athens the mother demands of her son!"
Rosily blushed the youth: he paused: but, lifting at length
His eyes from the ground, it seemed as he gathered the rest of his strength
Into the utterance—"Pan spoke thus: 'For what thou hast done
Count on a worthy reward! Henceforth be allowed thee release
From the racer's toil, no vulgar reward in praise or in pelf!'

"I am bold to believe, Pan means reward the most to my mind!
Fight I shall, with our foremost, wherever this fennel may grow,—
Pound—Pan helping us—Persia to dust, and, under the deep,
Whelm her away forever; and then,—no Athens to save,—
Marry a certain maid, I know keeps faith to the brave,—
Hie to my house and home: and, when my children shall creep
Close to my knees,—recount how the God was awful yet kind,
Promised their sire reward to the full—rewarding him—so!"

Unforeseeing one! Yes, he fought on the Marathon day:

So, when Persia was dust, all cried "To Akropolis!
Run, Pheidippides, one race more! the meed is thy due!
'Athens is saved, thank Pan,' go shout!" He flung down his shield,
Ran like fire once more: and the space 'twixt the Fennel-field
And Athens was stubble again, a field which a fire runs through,
Till in he broke: "Rejoice, we conquer!" Like wine through clay,
Joy in his blood bursting his heart, he died—the bliss!

So, to this day, when friend meets friend, the word of salute
Is still "Rejoice!"—his word which brought rejoicing indeed.
So is Pheidippides happy forever,—the noble strong man
Who could race like a god, bear the face of a god, whom a god loved so well;
He saw the land saved he had helped to save, and was suffered to tell
Such tidings, yet never decline, but, gloriously as he began,
So to end gloriously—once to shout, thereafter be mute:
"Athens is saved!"—Pheidippides dies in the shout for his meed.

HALBERT AND HOB

Here is a thing that happened. Like wild beasts whelped, for den,
In a wild part of North England, there lived once two wild men
Inhabiting one homestead, neither a hovel nor hut,
Time out of mind their birthright: father and son, these—but—
Such a son, such a father! Most wildness by degrees
Softens away: yet, last of their line, the wildest and worst were these.

Criminals, then? Why, no: they did not murder and rob;
But, give them a word, they returned a blow—old Halbert as young Hob:
Harsh and fierce of word, rough and savage of deed,
Hated or feared the more—who knows?—the genuine wild-beast breed.

Thus were they found by the few sparse folk of the countryside;
But how fared each with other? E'en beasts couch, hide by hide,
In a growling, grudged agreement: so, father and son aye curled
The closelier up in their den because the last of their kind in the world.

Still, beast irks beast on occasion. One Christmas night of snow,
Came father and son to words—such words! more cruel because the blow
To crown each word was wanting, while taunt matched gibe, and curse
Competed with oath in wager, like pastime in hell,—nay, worse:
For pastime turned to earnest, as up there sprang at last
The son at the throat of the father, seized him and held him fast.

"Out of this house you go!" (there followed a hideous oath)—
"This oven where now we bake, too hot to hold us both!
If there's snow outside, there's coolness: out with you, bide a spell

In the drift and save the sexton the charge of a parish shell!"

Now, the old trunk was tough, was solid as stump of oak
Untouched at the core by a thousand years: much less had its seventy broke
One whipcord nerve in the muscly mass from neck to shoulder-blade
Of the mountainous man, whereon his child's rash hand like a feather weighed.

Nevertheless at once did the mammoth shut his eyes,
Drop chin to breast, drop hands to sides, stand stiffened—arms and thighs
All of a piece—struck mute, much as a sentry stands,
Patient to take the enemy's fire: his captain so commands.

Whereat the son's wrath flew to fury at such sheer scorn
Of his puny strength by the giant eld thus acting the babe new-born:
And "Neither will this turn serve!" yelled he. "Out with you! Trundle, log!
If you cannot tramp and trudge like a man, try all-fours like a dog!"

Still the old man stood mute. So, logwise,—down to floor
Pulled from his fireside place, dragged on from hearth to door,—
Was he pushed, a very log, staircase along, until
A certain turn in the steps was reached, a yard from the house-door-sill.

Then the father opened eyes—each spark of their rage extinct,—
Temples, late black, dead-blanched,—right-hand with left-hand linked,—
He faced his son submissive; when slow the accents came,
They were strangely mild though his son's rash hand on his neck lay all the same.

"Hob, on just such a night of a Christmas long ago,
For such a cause, with such a gesture, did I drag—so—
My father down thus far: but, softening here, I heard
A voice in my heart, and stopped: you wait for an outer word,

"For your own sake, not mine, soften you too! Untrod
Leave this last step we reach, nor brave the finger of God!
I dared not pass its lifting: I did well. I nor blame
Nor praise you. I stopped here: and, Hob, do you the same!"

Straightway the son relaxed his hold of the father's throat.
They mounted, side by side, to the room again: no note
Took either of each, no sign made each to either: last
As first, in absolute silence, their Christmas-night they passed.

At dawn, the father sate on, dead, in the selfsame place,
With an outburst blackening still the old bad fighting-face:
But the son crouched all a-tremble like any lamb new-yeaned.

When he went to the burial, some one's staff he borrowed,—tottered and leaned.
But his lips were loose, not locked,—kept muttering, mumbling. "There!

At his cursing and swearing!" the youngsters cried: but the elders thought "In prayer."
A boy threw stones: he picked them up and stored them in his vest.

So tottered, muttered, mumbled he, till he died, perhaps found rest.
"Is there a reason in nature for these hard hearts?" O Lear,
That a reason out of nature must turn them soft, seems clear!

IVÀN IVÀNOVITCH

"They tell me, your carpenters," quoth I to my friend the Russ,
"Make a simple hatchet serve as a tool-box serves with us.
Arm but each man with his axe, 'tis a hammer and saw and plane
And chisel, and—what know I else? We should imitate in vain
The mastery wherewithal, by a flourish of just the adze,
He cleaves, clamps, dovetails in,—no need of our nails and brads,—
The manageable pine: 'tis said he could shave himself
With the axe,—so all adroit, now a giant and now an elf,
Does he work and play at once!"

Quoth my friend the Russ to me,
"Ay, that and more beside on occasion! It scarce may be
You never heard tell a tale told children, time out of mind,
By father and mother and nurse, for a moral that's behind,
Which children quickly seize. If the incident happened at all,
We place it in Peter's time when hearts were great not small,
Germanized, Frenchified. I wager 'tis old to you
As the story of Adam and Eve, and possibly quite as true."

In the deep of our land, 't is said, a village from out the woods
Emerged on the great main-road 'twixt two great solitudes.
Through forestry right and left, black verst and verst of pine,
From village to village runs the road's long wide bare line.
Clearance and clearance break the else-unconquered growth
Of pine and all that breeds and broods there, leaving loth
Man's inch of masterdom,—spot of life, spirt of fire,—
To star the dark and dread, lest right and rule expire
Throughout the monstrous wild, a-hungered to resume
Its ancient sway, suck back the world into its womb:
Defrauded by man's craft which clove from North to South
This highway broad and straight e'en from the Neva's mouth
To Moscow's gates of gold. So, spot of life and spirt
Of fire aforesaid, burn, each village death-begirt
By wall and wall of pine—unprobed undreamed abyss.

Early one winter morn, in such a village as this,
Snow-whitened everywhere except the middle road

Ice-roughed by track of sledge, there worked by his abode
Ivàn Ivànovitch, the carpenter, employed
On a huge shipmast trunk; his axe now trimmed and toyed
With branch and twig, and now some chop athwart the hole
Changed bole to billets, bared at once the sap and soul.
About him, watched the work his neighbors sheepskin-clad;
Each bearded mouth puffed steam, each gray eye twinkled glad
To see the sturdy arm which, never stopping play,
Proved strong man's blood still boils, freeze winter as he may.
Sudden, a burst of bells. Out of the road, on edge
Of the hamlet—horse's hoofs galloping. "How, a sledge?
What's here?" cried all as—in, up to the open space,
Workyard and market-ground, folk's common meeting-place,—
Stumbled on, till he fell, in one last bound for life,
A horse: and, at his heels, a sledge held—"Dmìtri's wife!
Back without Dmitri too! and children—where are they?
Only a frozen corpse!"

They drew it forth: then—"Nay,
Not dead, though like to die! Gone hence a month ago:
Home again, this rough jaunt—alone through night and snow—
What can the cause be? Hark—Droug, old horse, how he groans:
His day's done! Chafe away, keep chafing, for she moans:
She's coming to! Give here: see, motherkin, your friends!
Cheer up, all safe at home! Warm inside makes amends
For outside cold,—sup quick! Don't look as we were bears!
What is it startles you? What strange adventure stares
Up at us in your face? You know friends—which is which?
I'm Vàssili, he's Sergeì, Ivàn Ivànovitch"—

At the word, the woman's eyes, slow-wandering till they neared
The blue eyes o'er the bush of honey-colored beard,
Took in full light and sense and—torn to rags, some dream
Which hid the naked truth—O loud and long the scream
She gave, as if all power of voice within her throat
Poured itself wild away to waste in one dread note!
Then followed gasps and sobs, and then the steady flow
Of kindly tears: the brain was saved, a man might know.
Down fell her face upon the good friend's propping knee;
His broad hands smoothed her head, as fain to brush it free
From fancies, swarms that stung like bees unhived. He soothed—
"Loukèria, Loùscha!"—still he, fondling, smoothed and smoothed.
At last her lips formed speech.

"Ivàn, dear—you indeed!
You, just the same dear you! While I ... Oh, intercede,
Sweet Mother, with thy Son Almighty—let his might
Bring yesterday once more, undo all done last night!

But this time yesterday, Ivàn, I sat like you,
A child on either knee, and, dearer than the two,
A babe inside my arms, close to my heart—that's lost
In morsels o'er the snow! Father, Son, Holy Ghost,
Cannot you bring again my blessed yesterday?"

When no more tears would flow, she told her tale: this way.

"Maybe, a month ago,—was it not?—news came here,
They wanted, deeper down, good workmen fit to rear
A church and roof it in. 'We'll go,' my husband said:
'None understands like me to melt and mould their lead.'
So, friends here helped us off—Ivàn, dear, you the first!
How gay we jingled forth, all five—(my heart will burst)—
While Dmìtri shook the reins, urged Droug upon his track!

"Well, soon the month ran out, we just were coming back,
When yesterday—behold, the village was on fire!
Fire ran from house to house. What help, as, nigh and nigher,
The flames came furious? 'Haste,' cried Dmìtri, 'men must do
The little good man may: to sledge and in with you,
You and our three! We check the fire by laying flat
Each building in its path,—I needs must stay for that,—
But you ... no time for talk! Wrap round you every rug,
Cover the couple close,—you'll have the babe to hug.
No care to guide old Droug, he knows his way, by guess,
Once start him on the road: but chirrup, none the less!
The snow lies glib as glass and hard as steel, and soon
You'll have rise, fine and full, a marvel of a moon.
Hold straight up, all the same, this lighted twist of pitch!
Once home and with our friend Ivàn Ivànovitch,
All's safe: I have my pay in pouch, all's right with me,
So I but find as safe you and our precious three!
Off, Droug!'—because the flames had reached us, and the men
Shouted 'But lend a hand, Dmìtri—as good as ten!'

"So, in we bundled—I, and those God gave me once;
Old Droug, that's stiff at first, seemed youthful for the nonce:
He understood the case, galloping straight ahead.
Out came the moon: my twist soon dwindled, feebly red
In that unnatural day—yes, daylight, bred between
Moonlight and snow-light, lamped those grotto-depths which screen
Such devils from God's eye. Ah, pines, how straight you grow,
Nor bend one pitying branch, true breed of brutal snow!
Some undergrowth had served to keep the devils blind
While we escaped outside their border!

"Was that—wind?

Anyhow, Droug starts, stops, back go his ears, he snuffs,
Snorts,—never such a snort! then plunges, knows the sough's
Only the wind: yet, no—our breath goes up too straight!
Still the low sound,—less low, loud, louder, at a rate
There's no mistaking more! Shall I lean out—look—learn
The truth whatever it be? Pad, pad! At last, I turn—

"'T is the regular pad of the wolves in pursuit of the life in the sledge!
An army they are: close-packed they press like the thrust of a wedge:
They increase as they hunt: for I see, through the pine-trunks ranged each side,
Slip forth new fiend and fiend, make wider and still more wide
The four-footed steady advance. The foremost—none may pass:
They are elders and lead the line, eye and eye—green-glowing brass!
But a long way distant still. Droug, save us! He does his best:
Yet they gain on us, gain, till they reach,—one reaches ... How utter the rest?
O that Satan-faced first of the band! How he lolls out the length of his tongue,
How he laughs and lets gleam his white teeth! He is on me, his paws pry among
The wraps and the rags! O my pair, my twin-pigeons, lie still and seem dead!
Stepàn, he shall never have you for a meal,—here's your mother instead!
No, he will not be counselled—must cry, poor Stiòpka, so foolish! though first
Of my boy-brood, he was not the best: nay, neighbors have called him the worst:
He was puny, an undersized slip,—a darling to me, all the same!
But little there was to be praised in the boy, and a plenty to blame.
I loved him with heart and soul, yes—-but deal him a blow for a fault,
He would sulk for whole days. 'Foolish boy! lie still or the villain will vault,
Will snatch you from over my head!' No use! he cries, screams,—who can hold
Fast a boy in a frenzy of fear! It follows—as I foretold!
The Satan-face snatched and snapped: I tugged, I tore—and then
His brother too needs must shriek! If one must go, 't is men
The Tsar needs, so we hear, not ailing boys! Perhaps
My hands relaxed their grasp, got tangled in the wraps:
God, he was gone! I looked: there tumbled the cursed crew,
Each fighting for a share: too busy to pursue!
That's so far gain at least: Droug, gallop another verst
Or two, or three—God sends we beat them, arrive the first!
A mother who boasts two boys was ever accounted rich:
Some have not a boy: some have, but lose him,—God knows which
Is worse: how pitiful to see your weakling pine
And pale and pass away! Strong brats, this pair of mine!

"O misery! for while I settle to what near seems
Content, I am 'ware again of the tramp, and again there gleams—
Point and point—the line, eyes, levelled green brassy fire!
So soon is resumed your chase? Will nothing appease, naught tire
The furies? And yet I think—I am certain the race is slack,
And the numbers are nothing like. Not a quarter of the pack!
Feasters and those full-fed are staying behind ... Ah, why?
We'll sorrow for that too soon! Now,—gallop, reach home, and die,

Nor ever again leave house, to trust our life in the trap
For life—we call a sledge! Teriòscha, in my lap!
Yes, I'll lie down upon you, tight-tie you with the strings
Here—of my heart! No fear, this time, your mother flings ...
Flings? I flung? Never! But think!—a woman, after all,
Contending with a wolf! Save you I must and shall, Terentìì!
"How now? What, you still head the race,
Your eyes and tongue and teeth crave fresh food, Satan-face?
There and there! Plain I struck green fire out! Flash again?
All a poor fist can do to damage eyes proves vain!
My fist—why not crunch that? He is wanton for ... O God,
Why give this wolf his taste? Common wolves scrape and prod
The earth till out they scratch some corpse—mere putrid flesh!
Why must this glutton leave the faded, choose the fresh?
Terentìì—God, feel!—his neck keeps fast thy bag
Of holy things, saints' bones, this Satan-face will drag
Forth, and devour along with him, our Pope declared
The relics were to save from danger!

"Spurned, not spared!
'Twas through my arms, crossed arms, he—nuzzling now with snout,
Now ripping, tooth and claw—plucked, pulled Terentìì out,
A prize indeed! I saw—how could I else but see?—
My precious one—I bit to hold back—pulled from me!
Up came the others, fell to dancing—did the imps!—
Skipped as they scampered round. There's one is gray, and limps:
Who knows but old bad Màrpha—she always owed me spite
And envied me my births—skulks out of doors at night
And turns into a wolf, and joins the sisterhood,
And laps the youthful life, then slinks from out the wood,
Squats down at door by dawn, spins there demure as erst
—No strength, old crone,—not she!—to crawl forth half a verst!

"Well, I escaped with one: 'twixt one and none there lies
The space 'twixt heaven and hell. And see, a rose-light dyes
The endmost snow: 'tis dawn, 'tis day, 'tis safe at home!
We have outwitted you! Ay, monsters, snarl and foam,
Fight each the other fiend, disputing for a share,—
Forgetful, in your greed, our finest off we hear,
Tough Droug and I,—my babe, my boy that shall be man,
My man that shall be more, do all a hunter can
To trace and follow and find and catch and crucify
Wolves, wolfkins, all your crew! A thousand deaths shall die
The whimperingest cub that ever squeezed the teat!
'Take that!' we'll stab you with,—'the tenderness we met
When, wretches, you danced round,—not this, thank God—not this!
Hellhounds, we balk you!'

"But—Ah, God above!—Bliss, bliss,—
Not the band, no! And yet—yes, for Droug knows him! One—
This only of them all has said 'She saves a son!'
His fellows disbelieve such luck: but he believes,
He lets them pick the bones, laugh at him in their sleeves:
He 's off and after us,—one speck, one spot, one ball
Grows bigger, bound on bound,—one wolf as good as all!
Oh, but I know the trick! Have at the snaky tongue!
That 's the right way with wolves! Go, tell your mates I wrung
The panting morsel out, left you to howl your worst!
Now for it—now! Ah me! I know him—thrice-accurst
Satan-face,—him to the end my foe!

"All fight 's in vain:
This time the green brass points pierce to my very brain.
I fall—fall as I ought—quite on the babe I guard:
I overspread with flesh the whole of him. Too hard
To die this way, torn piecemeal? Move hence? Not I—one inch!
Gnaw through me, through and through: flat thus I lie nor flinch!
O God, the feel of the fang furrowing my shoulder!—see!
It grinds—it grates the bone. O Kìrill under me,
Could I do more? Besides he knew wolf's way to win:
I clung, closed round like wax: yet in he wedged and in,
Past my neck, past my breasts, my heart, until ... how feels
The onion-bulb your knife parts, pushing through its peels,
Till out you scoop its clove wherein lie stalk and leaf
And bloom and seed unborn?

"That slew me: yes, in brief,
I died then, dead I lay doubtlessly till Droug stopped
Here, I suppose. I come to life, I find me propped
Thus,—how or when or why—I know not. Tell me, friends,
All was a dream: laugh quick and say the nightmare ends!
Soon I shall find my house: 't is over there: in proof,
Save for that chimney heaped with snow, you 'd see the roof
Which holds my three—my two—my one—not one?

"Life 's mixed
With misery, yet we live—must live. The Satan fixed
His face on mine so fast, I took its print as pitch
Takes what it cools beneath. Ivàn Ivànovitch,
'T is you unharden me, you thaw, disperse the thing!
Only keep looking kind, the horror will not cling.
Your face smooths fast away each print of Satan. Tears
—What good they do! Life 's sweet, and all its after-years,
Ivàn Ivànovitch, I owe you! Yours am I!
May God reward you, dear!"

Down she sank. Solemnly
Ivàn rose, raised his axe,—for fitly, as she knelt,
Her head lay: well-apart, each side, her arms hung,—dealt
Lightning-swift thunder-strong one blow—no need of more!
Headless she knelt on still: that pine was sound at core
(Neighbors were used to say)—cast-iron-kernelled—which
Taxed for a second stroke Ivàn Ivànovitch.

The man was scant of words as strokes. "It had to be:
I could no other: God it was, bade 'Act for me!'"
Then stooping, peering round—what is it now he lacks?
A proper strip of bark wherewith to wipe his axe.
Which done, he turns, goes in, closes the door behind.
The others mute remain, watching the blood-snake wind
Into a hiding-place among the splinter-heaps.

At length, still mute, all move: one lifts—from where it steeps
Redder each ruddy rag of pine—the head: two more
Take up the dripping body: then, mute still as before,
Move in a sort of march, march on till marching ends
Opposite to the church; where halting,—who suspends,
By its long hair, the thing, deposits in its place
The piteous head: once more the body shows no trace
Of harm done: there lies whole the Loùscha, maid and wife
And mother, loved until this latest of her life.
Then all sit on the bank of snow which bounds a space
Kept free before the porch of judgment: just the place!

Presently all the souls, man, woman, child, which make
The village up, are found assembling for the sake
Of what is to be done. The very Jews are there:
A Gypsy-troop, though bound with horses for the Fair,
Squats with the rest. Each heart with its conception seethes
And simmers, but no tongue speaks: one may say,—none breathes.

Anon from out the church totters the Pope—the priest—
Hardly alive, so old, a hundred years at least.
With him, the Commune's head, a hoary senior too,
Stàrosta, that 's his style,—like Equity Judge with you,—
Natural Jurisconsult: then, fenced about with furs,
Pomeschìk,—Lord of the Land, who wields—and none demurs—
A power of life and death. They stoop, survey the corpse.

Then, straightened on his staff, the Stàrosta—the thorpe's
Sagaciousest old man—hears what you just have heard,
From Droug's first inrush, all, up to Ivàn's last word—
"God bade me act for him: I dared not disobey!"

Silence—the Pomeschìk broke with "A wild wrong way
Of righting wrong—if wrong there were, such wrath to rouse!
Why was not law observed? What article allows
Whoso may please to play the judge, and, judgment dealt,
Play executioner, as promptly as we pelt
To death, without appeal, the vermin whose sole fault
Has been—it dared to leave the darkness of its vault,
Intrude upon our day! Too sudden and too rash!
What was this woman's crime? Suppose the church should crash
Down where I stand, your lord: bound are my serfs to dare
Their utmost that I 'scape: yet, if the crashing scare
My children—as you are,—if sons fly, one and all,
Leave father to his fate,—poor cowards though I call
The runaways, I pause before I claim their life
Because they prized it more than mine. I would each wife
Died for her husband's sake, each son to save his sire:
'T is glory, I applaud—scarce duty, I require.
Ivàn Ivànovitch has done a deed that 's named
Murder by law and me: who doubts, may speak unblamed!"

All turned to the old Pope. "Ay, children, I am old—
How old, myself have got to know no longer. Rolled
Quite round, my orb of life, from infancy to age,
Seems passing back again to youth. A certain stage
At least I reach, or dream I reach, where I discern
Truer truths, laws behold more lawlike than we learn
When first we set our foot to tread the course I trod
With man to guide my steps: who leads me now is God.
'Your young men shall see visions:' and in my youth I saw
And paid obedience to man's visionary law:
'Your old men shall dream dreams:' and, in my age, a hand
Conducts me through the cloud round law to where I stand
Firm on its base,—know cause, who, before, knew effect.

"The world lies under me: and nowhere I detect
So great a gift as this—God's own—of human life.
'Shall the dead praise thee?' No! 'The whole live world is rife,
God, with thy glory,' rather! Life then, God's best of gifts,
For what shall man exchange? For life—when so he shifts
The weight and turns the scale, lets life for life restore
God's balance, sacrifice the less to gain the more,
Substitute—for low life, another's or his own—
Life large and liker God's who gave it: thus alone
May life extinguish life that life may trulier be!
How low this law descends on earth, is not for me
To trace: complexed becomes the simple, intricate
The plain, when I pursue law's winding. 'T is the straight
Outflow of law I know and name: to law, the fount

Fresh from God's footstool, friends, follow while I remount.

"A mother bears a child: perfection is complete
So far in such a birth. Enabled to repeat
The miracle of life,—herself was born so just
A type of womankind, that God sees fit to trust
Her with the holy task of giving life in turn.
Crowned by this crowning pride, how say you, should she spurn
Regality—discrowned, unchilded, by her choice
Of barrenness exchanged for fruit which made rejoice
Creation, though life's self were lost in giving birth
To life more fresh and fit to glorify God's earth?
How say you, should the hand God trusted with life's torch
Kindled to light the world—aware of sparks that scorch,
Let fall the same? Forsooth, her flesh a fire-flake stings:
The mother drops the child! Among what monstrous things
Shall she be classed? Because of motherhood, each male
Yields to his partner place, sinks proudly in the scale:
His strength owned weakness, wit—folly, and courage—fear,
Beside the female proved male's mistress—only here.
The fox-dam, hunger-pined, will slay the felon sire
Who dares assault her whelp: the beaver, stretched on fire,
Will die-without a groan: no pang avails to wrest
Her young from where they hide—her sanctuary breast.
What 's here then? Answer me, thou dead one, as, I trow,
Standing at God's own bar, he bids thee answer now!
Thrice crowned wast thou—each crown of pride, a child—thy charge!
Where are they? Lost? Enough: no need that thou enlarge
On how or why the loss: life left to utter 'lost'
Condemns itself beyond appeal. The soldier's post
Guards from the foe's attack the camp he sentinels:
That he no traitor proved, this and this only tells—
Over the corpse of him trod foe to foe's success.
Yet—one by one thy crowns torn from thee—thou no less
To scare the world, shame God,—livedst! I hold he saw
The unexampled sin, ordained the novel law,
Whereof first instrument was first intelligence
Found loyal here. I hold that, failing human sense,
The very earth had oped, sky fallen, to efface
Humanity's new wrong, motherhood's first disgrace.
Earth oped not, neither fell the sky, for prompt was found
A man and mar enough, head-sober and heart-sound,
Ready to hear God's voice, resolute to obey.
Ivàn Ivànovitch, I hold, has done, this day,
No otherwise than did, in ages long ago,
Moses when he made known the purport of that flow
Of fire athwart the law's twain-tables! I proclaim
Ivàn Ivànovitch God's servant!"

At which name
Uprose that creepy whisper from out the crowd, is wont,
To swell and surge and sink when fellow-men confront
A punishment that falls on fellow flesh and blood,
Appallingly beheld—shudderingly understood,
No less, to be the right, the just, the merciful.
"God's servant!" hissed the crowd.

When the Amen grew dull
And died away and left acquittal plain adjudged,
"Amen!" last sighed the lord. "There 's none shall say I grudged
Escape from punishment in such a novel case.
Deferring to old age and holy life,—be grace
Granted! say I. No less, scruples might shake a sense
Firmer than I boast mine. Law 's law, and evidence
Of breach therein lies plain,—blood-red-bright,—all may see!
Yet all absolve the deed: absolved the deed must be!

"And next—as mercy rules the hour—methinks 't were well
You signify forthwith its sentence, and dispel
The doubts and fears, I judge, which busy now the head
Law puts a halter round—a halo—you, instead!
Ivàn Ivànovitch—what think you he expects
Will follow from his feat? Go, tell him—law protects
Murder, for once: no need he longer keep behind
The Sacred Pictures—where skulks Innocence enshrined,
Or I missay! Go, some! You others, haste and hide
The dismal object there: get done, whate'er betide!"

So, while the youngers raised the corpse, the elders trooped
Silently to the house: where halting, some one stooped,
Listened beside the door; all there was silent too.
Then they held counsel; then pushed door and, passing through,
Stood in the murderer's presence.

Ivàn Ivànovitch
Knelt, building on the floor that Kremlin rare and rich
He deftly cut and carved on lazy winter nights.
Some five young faces watched, breathlessly, as, to rights,
Piece upon piece, he reared the fabric nigh complete.
Stèscha, Ivàn's old mother, sat spinning by the heat
Of the oven where his wife Kàtia stood baking bread.
Ivàn's self, as he turned his honey-colored head,
Was just in act to drop, 'twixt fir-cones,—each a dome,—
The scooped-out yellow gourd presumably the home
Of Kolokol the Big: the bell, therein to hitch,
—An acorn-cup—was ready: Ivàn Ivànovitch

Turned with it in his mouth.

They told him he was free
As air to walk abroad. "How otherwise?" asked he.

TRAY

This poem describes an actual incident witnessed in Paris by a friend of Browning's, and with accuracy of detail. The poem was written as a protest against vivisection, which the poet called "an infamous practice." He was early associated with Miss Frances Power Cobbe in her efforts to prevent vivisection; and he was a vice-president of the "Victoria Street Society for the Protection of Animals." Dr. Berdoe says, "He always expressed the utmost abhorrence of the practices which it opposes." To Miss Cobbe he wrote in 1874: "You have heard, 'I take an equal interest with yourself in the effort to suppress vivisection.' I dare not so honor my mere wishes and prayers as to put them for a moment beside your noble acts; but this I know, I would rather submit to the worst of deaths, so far as pain goes, than have a single dog or cat tortured on the pretence of sparing me a twinge or two." He goes even so far as to say that the person not willing to sign the petition against vivisection certainly could not be numbered among his friends. To Miss Stackpoole he wrote in April, 1883: "I despise and abhor the pleas on behalf of that infamous practice, vivisection." G. W. COOKE.

Sing me a hero! Quench my thirst
Of soul, ye bards!

Quoth Bard the first:
"Sir Olaf, the good knight, did don
His helm and eke his habergeon" ...
Sir Olaf and his bard—!

"That sin-scathed brow" (quoth Bard the second),
"That eye wide ope as though Fate beckoned
My hero to some steep, beneath
Which precipice smiled tempting death" ...
You too without your host have reckoned!

"A beggar-child" (let 's hear this third!)
"Sat on a quay's edge: like a bird
Sang to herself at careless play,
And fell into the stream. 'Dismay!
Help, you the standers-by!' None stirred.

"Bystanders reason, think of wives
And children ere they risk their lives.
Over the balustrade has bounced
A mere instinctive dog, and pounced
Plumb on the prize. 'How well he dives!

"'Up he comes with the child, see, tight
In mouth, alive too, clutched from quite
A depth of ten feet—twelve, I bet!
Good dog! What, off again? There 's yet
Another child to save? All right!'

"How strange we saw no other fall!
It 's instinct in the animal.
Good dog! But he 's a long while under:
If he got drowned I should not wonder—
Strong current, that against the wall!

"'Here he comes, holds in mouth this time
—What may the thing be? Well, that 's prime!
Now, did you ever? Reason reigns
In man alone, since all Tray's pains
Have fished—the child's doll from the slime!'

"And so, amid the laughter gay,
Trotted my hero off,—old Tray,—
Till somebody, prerogatived
With reason, reasoned: 'Why he dived,
His brain would show us, I should say.

"'John, go and catch—or, if needs be,
Purchase—that animal for me!
By vivisection, at expense
Of half-an-hour and eighteenpence,
How brain secretes dog's soul, we'll see!'"

NED BRATTS

Written from memory of Bunyan's story of old Tod in The Life and Death of Mr. Badman.

'T was Bedford Special Assize, one daft Midsummer's Day:
A broiling blasting June,—was never its like, men say.
Corn stood sheaf-ripe already, and trees looked yellow as that;
Ponds drained dust-dry, the cattle lay foaming around each flat.
Inside town, dogs went mad, and folk kept bibbing beer,
While the parsons prayed for rain. 'T was horrible, yes—but queer:
Queer—for the sun laughed gay, yet nobody moved a hand
To work one stroke at his trade: as given to understand
That all was come to a stop, work and such worldly ways,
And the world's old self about to end in a merry blaze,
Midsummer's day moreover was the first of Bedford Fair;
With Bedford Town's tag-rag and bobtail a-bowsing there.

But the Court House, Quality crammed: through doors ope, windows wide,
High on the Bench you saw sit Lordships side by side.
There frowned Chief Justice Jukes, fumed learned Brother Small,
And fretted their fellow Judge: like threshers, one and all,
Of a reek with laying down the law in a furnace. Why?
Because their lungs breathed flame—the regular crowd forbye—
From gentry pouring in—quite a nosegay, to be sure!
How else could they pass the time, six mortal hours endure
Till night should extinguish day, when matters might haply mend?
Meanwhile no bad resource was—watching begin and end
Some trial for life and death, in a brisk five minutes' space,
And betting which knave would 'scape, which hang, from his sort of face.

So, their Lordships toiled and moiled, and a deal of work was done
(I warrant) to justify the mirth of the crazy sun,
As this and t' other lout, struck dumb at the sudden show
Of red robes and white wigs, boggled nor answered "Boh!"
When asked why he, Tom Styles, should not—because Jack Nokes
Had stolen the horse—be hanged: for Judges must have their jokes,
And louts must make allowance—let 's say, for some blue fly
Which punctured a dewy scalp where the frizzles stuck awry—
Else Tom had fleered scot-free, so nearly over and done
Was the main of the job. Full-measure, the gentles enjoyed their fun,
As a twenty-five were tried, rank puritans caught at prayer
In a cow-house and laid by the heels,—have at 'em, devil may care!—
And ten were prescribed the whip, and ten a brand on the cheek,
And five a slit of the nose—just leaving enough to tweak.

Well, things at jolly high-tide, amusement steeped in fire,
While noon smote fierce the roof's red tiles to heart's desire,
The Court a-simmer with smoke, one ferment of oozy flesh,
One spirituous humming musk mount-mounting until its mesh
Entoiled all heads in a fluster, and Serjeant Postlethwayte
—Dashing the wig oblique as he mopped his oily pate—
Cried "Silence, or I grow grease! No loophole lets in air?
Jurymen,—Guilty, Death! Gainsay me if you dare!"
—Things at this pitch, I say,—what hubbub without the doors?
What laughs, shrieks, hoots and yells, what rudest of uproars?

Bounce through the barrier throng a bulk comes rolling vast!
Thumps, kicks,—no manner of use!—spite of them rolls at last
Into the midst a ball, which, bursting, brings to view
Publican Black Ned Bratts and Tabby his big wife too:
Both in a muck-sweat, both ... were never such eyes uplift
At the sight of yawning hell, such nostrils—snouts that sniffed
Sulphur, such mouths agape ready to swallow flame!
Horrified, hideous, frank fiend-faces! yet, all the same,

Mixed with a certain ... eh? how shall I dare style—mirth
The desperate grin of the guess that, could they break from earth,
Heaven was above, and hell might rage in impotence
Below the saved, the saved!

"Confound you! (no offence!)
Out of our way,—push, wife! Yonder their Worships be!"
Ned Bratts has reached the bar, and "Hey, my Lords," roars he,
"A Jury of life and death, Judges the prime of the land,
Constables, javelineers,—all met, if I understand,
To decide so knotty a point as whether 't was Jack or Joan
Robbed the henroost, pinched the pig, hit the King's Arms with a stone,
Dropped the baby down the well, left the tithesman in the lurch,
Or, three whole Sundays running, not once attended church!
What a pother—do these deserve the parish-stocks or whip,
More or less brow to brand, much or little nose to snip,—
When, in our Public, plain stand we—that 's we stand here
I and my Tab, brass-bold, brick-built of beef and beer,
—Do not we, slut? Step forth and show your beauty, jade!
Wife of my bosom—that 's the word now! What a trade
We drove! None said us nay: nobody loved his life
So little as wag a tongue against us,—did they, wife?
Yet they knew us all the while, in their hearts, for what we are
—Worst couple, rogue and quean, unhanged—search near and far!
Eh, Tab? The peddler, now—o'er his noggin—who warned a mate
To cut and run, nor risk his pack where its loss of weight
Was the least to dread,—aha, how we two laughed a-good
As, stealing round the midden, he came on where I stood
With billet poised and raised,—you, ready with the rope,—
Ah, but that 's past, that 's sin repented of, we hope!
Men knew us for that same, yet safe and sound stood we!
The lily-livered knaves knew too (I 've balked a d—)
Our keeping the 'Pied Bull' was just a mere pretence:
Too slow the pounds make food, drink, lodging, from out the pence!
There 's not a stoppage to travel has chanced, this ten long year,
No break into hall or grange, no lifting of nag or steer,
Not a single roguery, from the clipping of a purse
To the cutting of a throat, but paid us toll. Od's curse!
When Gypsy Smouch made bold to cheat us of our due,
—Eh, Tab? the Squire's strong-box we helped the rascal to—
I think he pulled a face, next Sessions' swinging-time!
He danced the jig that needs no floor,—and, here 's the prime,
'T was Scroggs that houghed the mare! Ay, those were busy days!

"Well, there we flourished brave, like scripture-trees called bays,
Faring high, drinking hard, in money up to head
—Not to say, boots and shoes, when ... Zounds, I nearly said—
Lord, to unlearn one's language! How shall we labor, wife?

Have you, fast hold, the Book? Grasp, grip it, for your life!
See, sirs, here 's life, salvation! Here 's—hold but out my breath—
When did I speak so long without once swearing? 'Sdeath,
No, nor unhelped by ale since man and boy! And yet
All yesterday I had to keep my whistle wet
While reading Tab this Book: book? don't say 'book'—they 're plays,
Songs, ballads, and the like: here 's no such strawy blaze,
But sky wide ope, sun, moon, and seven stars out full-flare!
Tab, help and tell! I 'm hoarse. A mug! or —no, a prayer!
Dip for one out of the Book! Who wrote it in the Jail
—He plied his pen unhelped by beer, sirs, I 'll be bail!

"I 've got my second wind. In trundles she—that 's Tab.
'Why, Gammer, what 's come now, that—bobbing like a crab
On Yule-tide bowl—your head 's a-work and both your eyes
Break loose? Afeard, you fool? As if the dead can rise!
Say—Bagman Dick was found last May with fuddling-cap
Stuffed in his month: to choke 's a natural mishap!'
'Gaffer, be—blessed,' cries she, 'and Bagman Dick as well!
I, you, and he are damned: this Public is our hell:
We live in fire: live coals don't feel!—once quenched, they learn—
Cinders do, to what dust they moulder while they burn!'

"'If you don't speak straight out,' says I—belike I swore—
'A knobstick, well you know the taste of, shall, once more,
Teach you to talk, my maid!' She ups with such a face,
Heart sunk inside me. 'Well, pad on, my prate-apace!'

"'I 've been about those laces we need for ... never mind!
If henceforth they tie hands, 't is mine they 'll have to bind.
You know who makes them best—the Tinker in our cage,
Pulled-up for gospelling, twelve years ago: no age
To try another trade,—yet, so he scorned to take
Money he did not earn, he taught himself the make
Of laces, tagged and tough—Dick Bagman found them so!
Good customers were we! Well, last week, you must know,
His girl,—the blind young chit, who hawks about his wares,—
She takes it in her head to come no more—such airs
These hussies have! Yet, since we need a stoutish lace,—
"I 'll to the jail-bird father, abuse her to his face!"
So, first I filled a jug to give me heart, and then,
Primed to the proper pitch, I posted to their den—
Patmore, they style their prison! I tip the turnkey, catch
My heart up, fix my face, and fearless lift the latch—
Both arms akimbo, in bounce with a good round oath
Ready for rapping out: no "Lawks" nor "By my troth!"

"'There sat my man, the father. He looked up: what one feels

When heart that leapt to mouth drops down again to heels!
He raised his hand ... Hast seen, when drinking out the night,
And in, the day, earth grow another something quite
Under the sun's first stare? I stood a very stone.

"""Woman!" (a fiery tear he put in every tone),
"How should my child frequent your house where lust is sport,
Violence—trade? Too true! I trust no vague report.
Her angel's hand, which stops the sight of sin, leaves clear
The other gate of sense, lets outrage through the ear.
What has she heard!—which, heard shall never be again.
Better lack food than feast, a Dives in the—wain
Or reign or train—of Charles!" (His language was not ours:
'T is my belief, God spoke: no tinker has such powers.)
"Bread, only bread they bring—my laces: if we broke
Your lump of leavened sin, the loaf's first crumb would choke!"

"'Down on my marrow-bones! Then all at once rose he:
His brown hair burst a-spread, his eyes were suns to see:
Up went his hands: "Through flesh, I reach, I read thy soul!
So may some stricken tree look blasted, bough and bole,
Champed by the fire-tooth, charred without, and yet, thrice-bound
With dreriment about, within may life be found,
A prisoned power to branch and blossom as before,
Could but the gardener cleave the cloister, reach the core,
Loosen the vital sap: yet where shall help be found?
Who says 'How save it?'—nor 'Why cumbers it the ground?'
Woman, that tree art thou! All sloughed about with scurf,
Thy stag-horns fright the sky, thy snake-roots sting the turf!
Drunkenness, wantonness, theft, murder gnash and gnarl
Thine outward, case thy soul with coating like the marle
Satan stamps flat upon each head beneath his hoof!
And how deliver such? The strong men keep aloof,
Lover and friend stand far, the mocking ones pass by,
Tophet gapes wide for prey: lost soul, despair and die!
What then? 'Look unto me and be ye saved!' saith God:
'I strike the rock, outstreats the life-stream at my rod!
Be your sins scarlet, wool shall they seem like, —although
As crimson red, yet turn white as the driven snow!'"

"'There, there, there! All I seem to somehow understand
Is—that, if I reached home, 't was through the guiding hand
Of his blind girl which led and led me through the streets
And out of town and up to door again. What greets
First thing my eye, as limbs recover from their swoon?
A book—this Book she gave at parting. "Father's boon—
The Book he wrote: it reads as if he spoke himself:
He cannot preach in bonds, so,—take it down from shelf

When you want counsel,—think you hear his very voice!

"'Wicked dear Husband, first despair and then rejoice!
Dear wicked Husband, waste no tick of moment more,
Be saved like me, bald trunk! There 's greenness yet at core,
Sap under slough! Read, read!'

"Let me take breath, my lords!
I 'd like to know, are these—hers, mine, or Bunyan's words?
I 'm 'wildered—scarce with drink,—nowise with drink alone!
You 'll say, with heat: but heat 's no stuff to split a stone
Like this black boulder—this flint heart of mine: the Book—
That dealt the crashing blow! Sirs, here 's the fist that shook
His beard till Wrestler Jem howled like a just-lugged bear!
You had brained me with a feather: at once I grew aware
Christmas was meant for me. A burden at your back,
Good Master Christmas? Nay,—yours was that Joseph's sack,
—Or whose it was,—which held the cup,—compared with mine!
Robbery loads my loins, perjury cracks my chine,
Adultery ... nay, Tab, you pitched me as I flung!
One word, I 'll up with fist ... No, sweet spouse, hold your tongue!

"I 'm hasting to the end. The Book, sirs—take and read!
You have my history in a nutshell,—ay, indeed!
It must off, my burden! See,—slack straps and into pit,
Roll, reach the bottom, rest, rot there—a plague on it!
For a mountain 's sure to fall and bury Bedford Town,
'Destruction'—that 's the name, and fire shall burn it down!
Oh, 'scape the wrath in time! Time 's now, if not too late.
How can I pilgrimage up to the wicket-gate?
Next comes Despond the slough: not that I fear to pull
Through mud, and dry my clothes at brave House Beautiful—
But it 's late in the day, I reckon: had I left years ago
Town, wife, and children dear ... Well, Christmas did, you know!—
Soon I had met in the valley and tried my cudgel's strength
On the enemy horned and winged, a-straddle across its length!
Have at his horns, thwick—thwack: they snap, see! Hoof and hoof—
Bang, break the fetlock-bones! For love's sake, keep aloof
Angels! I 'm man and match,—this cudgel for my flail,—
To thresh him, hoofs and horns, bat's wing and serpent's tail!
A chance gone by! But then, what else does Hopeful ding
Into the deafest ear except—hope, hope 's the thing?
Too late i' the day for me to thrid the windings: but
There 's still a way to win the race by death's short cut!
Did Master Faithful need climb the Delightful Mounts?
No, straight to Vanity Fair,—a fair, by all accounts,
Such as is held outside,—lords, ladies, grand and gay,—
Says he in the face of them, just what you hear me say.

And the Judges brought him in guilty, and brought him out
To die in the market-place—St. Peter's Green 's about
The same thing: there they flogged, flayed, buffeted, lanced with knives,
Pricked him with swords,—I 'll swear, he 'd full a cat's nine lives,—
So to his end at last came Faithful,—ha, ha, he!
Who holds the highest card? for there stands hid, you see,
Behind the rabble-rout, a chariot, pair and all:
He 's in, he 's off, he 's up, through clouds, at trumpet-call,
Carried the nearest way to Heaven-gate-! Odds my life—
Has nobody a sword to spare? not even a knife?
Then hang me, draw and quarter! Tab—do the same by her!
O Master Worldly-Wiseman ... that 's Master Interpreter,
Take the will, not the deed! Our gibbet 's handy, close:
Forestall Last Judgment-Day! Be kindly, not morose!
There wants no earthly judge-and-jurying: here we stand—
Sentence our guilty selves: so, hang us out of hand!
Make haste for pity's sake! A single moment's loss
Means—Satan 's lord once more: his whisper shoots across
All singing in my heart, all praying in my brain,
'It comes of heat and beer!'—hark how he guffaws plain!
'To-morrow you 'll wake bright, and, in a safe skin, hug
Your sound selves, Tab and you, over a foaming jug!
You 've had such qualms before, time out of mind!' He 's right!
Did not we kick and cuff and curse away, that night
When home we blindly reeled, and left poor humpback Joe
I' the lurch to pay for what ... somebody did, you know!
Both of us maundered then, 'Lame humpback,—never more
Will he come limping, drain his tankard at our door!
He 'll swing, while—somebody' ... Says Tab, 'No, for I 'll peach!'
'I 'm for you, Tab,' cries I, 'there 's rope enough for each!'
So blubbered we, and bussed, and went to bed upon
The grace of Tab's good thought: by morning, all was gone!
We laughed—'What 's life to him, a cripple of no account?'
Oh, waves increase around—I feel them mount and mount!
Hang us! To-morrow brings Tom Bearward with his bears:
One new black-muzzled brute beats Sackerson, he swears:
(Sackerson, for my money!) And, baiting o'er, the Brawl
They lead on Turner's Patch,—lads, lasses, up tails all,—
I 'm i' the thick o' the throng! That means the Iron Cage,
—Means the Lost Man inside! Where 's hope for such as wage
War against light? Light 's left, light 's here, I hold light still,
So does Tab—make but haste to hang us both! You will?"

I promise, when he stopped you might have heard a mouse
Squeak, such a death-like hush sealed up the old Mote House.
But when the mass of man sank meek upon his knees,
While Tab, alongside, wheezed a hoarse "Do hang us, please!"
Why, then the waters rose, no eye but ran with tears,

Hearts heaved, heads thumped, until, paying all past arrears
Of pity and sorrow, at last a regular scream outbroke
Of triumph, joy, and praise.

My Lord Chief Justice spoke,
First mopping brow and cheek, where still, for one that budged,
Another bead broke fresh: "What Judge, that ever judged
Since first the world began, judged such a case as this?
Why, Master Bratts, long since, folks smelt you out, I wis!
I had my doubts, i' faith, each time you played the fox
Convicting geese of crime in yonder witness-box—
Yea, much did I misdoubt, the thief that stole her eggs
Was hardly goosey's self at Reynard's game, i' feggs!
Yet thus much was to praise—you spoke to point, direct—
Swore you heard, saw the theft: no jury could suspect—
Dared to suspect,—I 'll say,—a spot in white so clear:
Goosey was throttled, true: but thereof godly fear
Came of example set, much as our laws intend;
And, though a fox confessed, you proved the Judge's friend.
What if I had my doubts? Suppose I gave them breath,
Brought you to bar: what work to do, ere 'Guilty, Death'
Had paid our pains! What heaps of witnesses to drag
From holes and corners, paid from out the County's bag!
Trial three dog-days long! Amicus Curiæ—that 's
Your title, no dispute—truth-telling Master Bratts!
Thank you, too, Mistress Tab! Why doubt one word you say?
Hanging you both deserve, hanged both shall be this day!
The tinker needs must be a proper man. I 've heard
He lies in Jail long since: if Quality's good word
Warrants me letting loose,—some householder, I mean—
Freeholder, better still,—I don't say but—between
Now and next Sessions ... Well! Consider of his case,
I promise to, at least: we owe him so much grace.
Not that—no, God forbid!—I lean to think as you,
The grace that such repent is any jail-bird's due:
I rather see the fruit of twelve years' pious reign—
Astræa Redux, Charles restored his rights again!
—Of which, another time! I somehow feel a peace
Stealing across the world. May deeds like this increase!
So, Master Sheriff, stay that sentence I pronounced
On those two dozen odd: deserving to be trounced
Soundly, and yet ... well, well, at all events dispatch
This pair of—shall I say, sinner-saints?—ere we catch
Their jail-distemper too. Stop tears, or I 'll indite
All weeping Bedfordshire for turning Bunyanite!"

So, forms were galloped through. If Justice, on the spur,
Proved somewhat expeditious, would Quality demur?

And happily hanged were they,—why lengthen out my tale?—
Where Bunyan's Statue stands facing where stood his Jail.

SECOND SERIES

"You are sick, that 's sure,"—they say:
"Sick of what?"—they disagree.
"'T is the brain,"—thinks Doctor A;
"'T is the heart,"—holds Doctor B;
"The liver—my life I 'd lay!"
"The lungs!" "The lights!"
Ah me!
So ignorant of man's whole
Of bodily organs plain to see—
So sage and certain, frank and free,
About what 's under lock and key—
Man's soul!

ECHETLOS

Here is a story, shall stir you! Stand up, Greeks dead and gone,
Who breasted, beat Barbarians, stemmed Persia rolling on,
Did the deed and saved the world, for the day was Marathon!

No man but did his manliest, kept rank and fought away
In his tribe and file: up, back, out, down—was the spear-arm play:
Like a wind-whipt branchy wood, all spear-arms a-swing that day!

But one man kept no rank, and his sole arm plied no spear,
As a flashing came and went, and a form i' the van, the rear,
Brightened the battle up, for he blazed now there, now here.

Nor helmed nor shielded, he! but, a goat-skin all his wear,
Like a tiller of the soil, with a clown's limbs broad and bare,
Went he ploughing on and on: he pushed with a ploughman's share.

Did the weak mid-line give way, as tunnies on whom the shark
Precipitates his bulk? Did the right-wing halt when, stark
On his heap of slain lay stretched Kallimachos Polemarch?

Did the steady phalanx falter? To the rescue, at the need,
The clown was ploughing Persia, clearing Greek earth of weed,
As he routed through the Sakian and rooted up the Mede.

But the deed done, battle won,—nowhere to be descried
On the meadow, by the stream, at the marsh, —look far and wide
From the foot of the mountain, no, to the last blood-plashed sea-side,—

Not anywhere on view blazed the large limbs thonged and brown,
Shearing and clearing still with the share before which—down
To the dust went Persia's pomp, as he ploughed for Greece, that clown!

How spake the Oracle? "Care for no name at all!
Say but just this: 'We praise one helpful whom we call
The Holder of the Ploughshare.' The great deed ne'er grows small."

Not the great name! Sing—woe for the great name Miltiadés
And its end at Paros isle! Woe for Themistokles
—Satrap in Sardis court! Name not the clown like these!

CLIVE

Browning had this story from Mrs. Jameson as early as 1846, she in turn having just heard Macaulay tell it. Browning's own narrative preceded Clive's death by a week only.

I and Clive were friends—and why not? Friends! I think you laugh, my lad.
Clive it was gave England India, while your father gives—egad,
England nothing but the graceless boy who lures him on to speak—
"Well, Sir, you and Clive were comrades—" with a tongue thrust in your cheek!
Very true: in my eyes, your eyes, all the world's eyes, Clive was man,
I was, am, and ever shall be—mouse, nay, mouse of all its clan
Sorriest sample, if you take the kitchen's estimate for fame;
While the man Clive—he fought Plassy, spoiled the clever foreign game,
Conquered and annexed and Englished!

Never mind! As o'er my punch
(You away) I sit of evenings,—silence, save for biscuit crunch,
Black, unbroken,—thought grows busy, thrids each pathway of old years,
Notes this forthright, that meander, till the long-past life appears
Like an outspread map of country plodded through, each mile and rood,
Once, and well remembered still,—I 'm startled in my solitude
Ever and anon by—what 's the sudden mocking light that breaks
On me as I slap the table till no rummer-glass but shakes
While I ask—aloud, I do believe, God help me!—"Was it thus?
Can it be that so I faltered, stopped when just one step for us—"
(Us,—you were not born, I grant, but surely some day born would be)
"—One bold step had gained a province" (figurative talk, you see)
"Got no end of wealth and honor,—yet I stood stock-still no less?"
—"For I was not Clive," you comment: but it needs no Clive to guess

Wealth were handy, honor ticklish, did no writing on the wall
Warn me "Trespasser, 'ware man-traps!" Him who braves that notice—call
Hero! none of such heroics suit myself who read plain words,
Doff my hat, and leap no barrier. Scripture says, the land 's the Lord's:
Louts then—what avail the thousand, noisy in a smock-frocked ring,
All-agog to have me trespass, clear the fence, be Clive their king?
Higher warrant must you show me ere I set one foot before
T' other in that dark direction, though I stand forevermore
Poor as Job and meek as Moses. Evermore? No! By and by
Job grows rich and Moses valiant, Clive turns out less wise than I.
Don't object "Why call him friend, then?" Power is power, my boy, and still
Marks a man,—God's gift magnific, exercised for good or ill.
You 've your boot now on my hearth-rug, tread what was a tiger's skin:
Rarely such a royal monster as I lodged the bullet in!
True, he murdered half a village, so his own death came to pass;
Still, for size and beauty, cunning, courage—ah, the brute he was!
Why, that Clive,—that youth, that greenhorn, that quill-driving clerk, in fine,—
He sustained a siege in Arcot ... But the world knows! Pass the wine.

Where did I break off at? How bring Clive in? Oh, you mentioned "fear"!
Just so: and, said I, that minds me of a story you shall hear.

We were friends then, Clive and I: so, when the clouds, about the orb
Late supreme, encroaching slowly, surely, threatened to absorb
Ray by ray its noontide brilliance,—friendship might, with steadier eye
Drawing near, bear what had burned else, now no blaze—all majesty.
Too much bee's-wing floats my figure? Well, suppose a castle 's new:
None presume to climb its ramparts, none find foothold sure for shoe
'Twixt those squares and squares of granite plating the impervious pile
As his scale-mail's warty iron cuirasses a crocodile.
Reels that castle thunder-smitten, storm-dismantled? From without
Scrambling up by crack and crevice, every cockney prates about
Towers—the heap he kicks now! turrets—just the measure of his cane!
Will that do? Observe moreover—(same similitude again)—
Such a castle seldom crumbles by sheer stress of cannonade:
'T is when foes are foiled and fighting 's finished that vile rains invade,
Grass o'ergrows, o'ergrows till night-birds congregating find no holes
Fit to build in like the topmost sockets made for banner-poles.
So Clive crumbled slow in London, crashed at last.

A week before,
Dining with him,—after trying churchyard chat of days of yore,—
Both of us stopped, tired as tombstones, headpiece, foot-piece, when they lean
Each to other, drowsed in fog-smoke, o'er a coffined Past between.
As I saw his head sink heavy, guessed the soul's extinguishment
By the glazing eyeball, noticed how the furtive fingers went
Where a drug-box skulked behind the honest liquor,—"One more throw
Try for Clive!" thought I: "Let 's venture some good rattling question!" So—

"Come Clive, tell us"—out I blurted—"what to tell in turn, years hence,
When my boy—suppose I have one—asks me on what evidence
I maintain my friend of Plassy proved a warrior every whit
Worth your Alexanders, Cæsars, Marlboroughs and—what said Pitt?—
Frederick the Fierce himself! Clive told me once"—I want to say—
"Which feat out of all those famous doings bore the bell away
—In his own calm estimation, mark you, not the mob's rough guess—
Which stood foremost as evincing what Clive called courageousness!
Come! what moment of the minute, what speck-centre in the wide
Circle of the action saw your mortal fairly deified?
(Let alone that filthy sleep-stuff, swallow bold this wholesome Port!)
If a friend has leave to question,—when were you most brave, in short?"

Up he arched his brows o' the instant—formidably Clive again.
"When was I most brave? I 'd answer, were the instance half as plain
As another instance that 's a brain-lodged crystal —curse it!—here
Freezing when my memory touches—ugh!—the time I felt most fear.
Ugh! I cannot say for certain if I showed fear—anyhow,
Fear I felt, and, very likely, shuddered, since I shiver now."

"Fear!" smiled I. "Well, that 's the rarer: that 's a specimen to seek,
Ticket up in one's museum, Mind-Freaks, Lord Clive's Fear, Unique!"

Down his brows dropped. On the table painfully he pored as though
Tracing, in the stains and streaks there, thoughts encrusted long ago.
When he spoke 't was like a lawyer reading word by word some will,
Some blind jungle of a statement,—beating on and on until
Out there leaps fierce life to fight with.

"This fell in my factor-days.
Desk-drudge, slaving at Saint David's, one must game, or drink, or craze.
I chose gaming: and,—because your high-flown gamesters hardly take
Umbrage at a factor's elbow if the factor pays his stake,—
I was winked at in a circle where the company was choice,
Captain This and Major That, men high of color, loud of voice,
Yet indulgent, condescending to the modest juvenile
Who not merely risked but lost his hard-earned guineas with a smile.

"Down I sat to cards, one evening,—had for my antagonist
Somebody whose name 's a secret—you 'll know why—so, if you list,
Call him Cock o' the Walk, my scarlet son of Mars from head to heel!
Play commenced: and, whether Cocky fancied that a clerk must feel
Quite sufficient honor came of bending over one green baize,
I the scribe with him the warrior, guessed no penman dared to raise
Shadow of objection should the honor stay but playing end
More or less abruptly,—whether disinclined he grew to spend
Practice strictly scientific on a booby born to stare
At—not ask of—lace-and-ruffles if the hand they hide plays fair,—

Anyhow, I marked a movement when he bade me 'Cut!'

"I rose.
'Such the new manœuvre, Captain? I'm a novice: knowledge grows.
What, you force a card, you cheat, Sir?'

"Never did a thunder-clap
Cause emotion, startle Thyrsis locked with Chloe in his lap,
As my word and gesture (down I flung my cards to join the pack)
Fired the man of arms, whose visage, simply red before, turned black.

When he found his voice, he stammered 'That expression once again!'

"'Well, you forced a card and cheated!'

"'Possibly a factor's brain,
Busied with his all-important balance of accounts, may deem
Weighing words superfluous trouble: cheat to clerkly ears may seem
Just the joke for friends to venture: but we are not friends, you see!
When a gentleman is joked with,—if he 's good at repartee,
He rejoins, as do I—Sirrah, on your knees, withdraw in full!
Beg my pardon, or be sure a kindly bullet through your skull
Lets in light and teaches manner to what brain it finds! Choose quick—
Have your life snuffed out or, kneeling, pray me trim yon candle-wick!'

"'Well, you cheated!'
"Then outbroke a howl from all the friends around.
To his feet sprang each in fury, fists were clenched and teeth were ground.
'End it! no time like the present! Captain, yours were our disgrace!
No delay, begin and finish! Stand back, leave the pair a space!
Let civilians be instructed: henceforth simply ply the pen,
Fly the sword! This clerk 's no swordsman? Suit him with a pistol, then!
Even odds! A dozen paces 'twixt the most and least expert
Make a dwarf a giant's equal: nay, the dwarf, if he 's alert,
Likelier hits the broader target!'

"Up we stood accordingly.
As they handed me the weapon, such was my soul's thirst to try
Then and there conclusions with this bully, tread on and stamp out
Every spark of his existence, that,—crept close to, curled about
By that toying tempting teasing fool-forefinger's middle joint,—
Don't you guess?—the trigger yielded. Gone my chance! and at the point
Of such prime success moreover: scarce an inch above his head
Went my ball to hit the wainscot. He was living, I was dead.

"Up he marched in flaming triumph—'t was his right, mind!—up, within
Just an arm's length. 'Now, my clerkling,' chuckled Cocky with a grin
As the levelled piece quite touched me, 'Now, Sir Counting-House, repeat

That expression which I told you proved bad manners! Did I cheat?'

"'Cheat you did, you knew you cheated, and, this moment, know as well.
As for me, my homely breeding bids you—fire and go to Hell!'

"Twice the muzzle touched my forehead. Heavy barrel, flurried wrist,
Either spoils a steady lifting. Thrice: then, 'Laugh at Hell who list,
I can't! God 's no fable either. Did this boy's eye wink once? No!
There 's no standing him and Hell and God all three against me,—so,
I did cheat!'

"And down he threw the pistol, out rushed—by the door
Possibly, but, as for knowledge if by chimney, roof or floor,
He effected disappearance—I 'll engage no glance was sent
That way by a single starer, such a blank astonishment
Swallowed up their senses: as for speaking—mute they stood as mice.

"Mute not long, though! Such reaction, such a hubbub in a trice!
'Rogue and rascal! Who 'd have thought it? What 's to be expected next,
When His Majesty's Commission serves a sharper as pretext
For ... But where 's the need of wasting time now? Naught requires delay:
Punishment the Service cries for: let disgrace be wiped away
Publicly, in good broad daylight! Resignation? No, indeed!
Drum and fife must play the Rogue's-March, rank and file be free to speed
Tardy marching on the rogue's part by appliance in the rear
—Kicks administered shall right this wronged civilian,—never fear,
Mister Clive, for—though a clerk—you bore yourself—suppose we say—
Just as would beseem a soldier?

"'Gentlemen, attention—pray!
First, one word!'

"I passed each speaker severally in review.
When I had precise their number, names and styles, and fully knew
Over whom my supervision thenceforth must extend,—why, then—

"'Some five minutes since, my life lay—as you all saw, gentlemen—
At the mercy of your friend there. Not a single voice was raised
In arrest of judgment, not one tongue—before my powder blazed—
Ventured "Can it be the youngster blundered, really seemed to mark
Some irregular proceeding? We conjecture in the dark,
Guess at random,—still, for sake of fair play—what if for a freak,
In a fit of absence,—such things have been!—if our friend proved weak
—What 's the phrase?—corrected fortune! Look into the case, at least!"
Who dared interpose between the altar's victim and the priest?
Yet he spared me! You eleven! Whosoever, all or each,
To the disadvantage of the man who spared me, utters speech
—To his face, behind his back,—that speaker has to do with me:

Me who promise, if positions change and mine the chance should be,
Not to imitate your friend and waive advantage!'

"Twenty-five
Years ago this matter happened: and 't is certain," added Clive,
"Never, to my knowledge, did Sir Cocky have a single breath
Breathed against him: lips were closed throughout his life, or since his death,
For if he be dead or living I can tell no more than you.
All I know is—Cocky had one chance more; how he used it,—grew
Out of such unlucky habits, or relapsed, and back again
Brought the late-ejected devil with a score more in his train,—
That 's for you to judge. Reprieval I procured, at any rate.
Ugh—the memory of that minute's fear makes gooseflesh rise! Why prate
Longer? You 've my story, there 's your instance: fear I did, you see!"

"Well"—I hardly kept from laughing—"if I see it, thanks must be
Wholly to your Lordship's candor. Not that —in a common case—
When a bully caught at cheating thrusts a pistol in one's face,
I should under-rate, believe me, such a trial to the nerve!
'T is no joke, at one-and-twenty, for a youth to stand nor swerve.
Fear I naturally look for—unless, of all men alive,
I am forced to make exception when I come to Robert Clive.
Since at Arcot, Plassy, elsewhere, he and death—the whole world knows—
Came to somewhat closer quarters."

Quarters? Had we come to blows,
Clive and I, you had not wondered—up he sprang so, out he rapped
Such a round of oaths—no matter! I 'll endeavor to adapt
To our modern usage words he—well, 't was friendly license—flung
At me like so many fire-balls, fast as he could wag his tongue.

"You—a soldier? You—at Plassy? Yours the faculty to nick
Instantaneously occasion when your foe, if lightning-quick,
—At his mercy, at his malice,—has you, through some stupid inch
Undefended in your bulwark? Thus laid open,—not to flinch
—That needs courage, you 'll concede me. Then, look here! Suppose the man.
Checking his advance, his weapon still extended, not a span
Distant from my temple,—curse him!—quietly had bade me, 'There!
Keep your life, calumniator!—worthless life I freely spare:
Mine you freely would have taken—murdered me and my good fame
Both at once—and all the better! Go, and thank your own bad aim
Which permits me to forgive you!' What if, with such words as these,
He had cast away his weapon? How should I have borne me, please?
Nay, I 'll spare you pains and tell you. This, and only this, remained—
Pick his weapon up and use it on myself. If so had gained
Sleep the earlier, leaving England probably to pay on still
Rent and taxes for half India, tenant at the Frenchman's will."

"Such the turn," said I, "the matter takes with you? Then I abate
—No, by not one jot nor tittle,—of your act my estimate.
Fear—I wish I could detect there: courage fronts me, plain enough—
Call it desperation, madness—never mind! for here 's in rough
Why, had mine been such a trial, fear had overcome disgrace.
True, disgrace were hard to bear: but such a rush against God's face
—None of that for me, Lord Plassy, since I go to church at times,
Say the creed my mother taught me! Many years in foreign climes
Rub some marks away—not all, though! We poor sinners reach life's brink,
Overlook what rolls beneath it, recklessly enough, but think
There 's advantage in what 's left us—ground to stand on, time to call
'Lord, have mercy!' ere we topple over—do not leap, that 's all!"

Oh, he made no answer, re-absorbed into his cloud. I caught
Something like "Yes—courage: only fools will call it fear."

If aught
Comfort you, my great unhappy hero Clive, in that I heard,
Next week, how your own hand dealt you doom, and uttered just the word
"Fearfully courageous!"—this, be sure, and nothing else I groaned.
I 'm no Clive, nor parson either: Clive's worst deed—we 'll hope condoned.

MULÉYKEH

If a stranger passed the tent of Hóseyn, he cried "A churl's!"
Or haply "God help the man who has neither salt nor bread!"
—"Nay," would a friend exclaim, "he needs nor pity nor scorn
More than who spends small thought on the shore-sand, picking pearls,
—Holds but in light esteem the seed-sort, bears instead
On his breast a moon-like prize, some orb which of night makes morn.

"What if no flocks and herds enrich the son of Sinán?
They went when his tribe was mulct, ten thousand camels the due,
Blood-value paid perforce for a murder done of old.
'God gave them, let them go! But never since time began,
Muléykeh, peerless mare, owned master the match of you,
And you are my prize, my Pearl: I laugh at men's land and gold!'

"So in the pride of his soul laughs Hóseyn—and right, I say.
Do the ten steeds run a race of glory? Outstripping all,
Ever Muléykeh stands first steed at the victor's staff.
Who started, the owner's hope, gets shamed and named, that day.
'Silence,' or, last but one, is 'The Cuffed,' as we use to call
Whom the paddock's lord thrusts forth. Right, Hóseyn, I say, to laugh!"

"Boasts he Muléykeh the Pearl?" the stranger replies: "Be sure

On him I waste nor scorn nor pity, but lavish both
On Duhl the son of Sheybán, who withers away in heart
For envy of Hóseyn's luck. Such sickness admits no cure.
A certain poet has sung, and sealed the same with an oath,
'For the vulgar—flocks and herds! The Pearl is a prize apart.'"

Lo, Duhl the son of Sheyban comes riding to Hoséyn's tent,
And he casts his saddle down, and enters and "Peace!" bids he.
"You are poor, I know the cause: my plenty shall mend the wrong.
'T is said of your Pearl—the price of a hundred camels spent
In her purchase were scarce ill paid: such prudence is far from me
Who proffer a thousand. Speak! Long parley may last too long."

Said Hóseyn, "You feed young beasts a many, of famous breed,
Slit-eared, unblemished, fat, true offspring of Múzennem:
There stumbles no weak-eyed she in the line as it climbs the hill.
But I love Muléykeh's face: her forefront whitens indeed
Like a yellowish wave's cream-crest. Your camels—go gaze on them!
Her fetlock is foam-splashed too. Myself am the richer still."

A year goes by: lo, back to the tent again rides Duhl.
"You are open-hearted, ay—moist-handed, a very prince.
Why should I speak of sale? Be the mare your simple gift!
My son is pined to death for her beauty: my wife prompts 'Fool,
Beg for his sake the Pearl! Be God the rewarder, since
God pays debts seven for one: who squanders on Him shows thrift,'"

Said Hóseyn, "God gives each man one life, like a lamp, then gives
That lamp due measure of oil: lamp lighted—hold high, wave wide
Its comfort for others to share! once quench it, what help is left?
The oil of your lamp is your son: I shine while Muléykeh lives.
Would I beg your son to cheer my dark if Muléykeh died?
It is life against life: what good avails to the life-bereft?"

Another year, and—hist! What craft is it Duhl designs?
He alights not at the door of the tent as he did last time,
But, creeping behind, he gropes his stealthy way by the trench
Half-round till he finds the flap in the folding, for night combines
With the robber—and such is he: Duhl, covetous up to crime,
Must wring from Hóseyn's grasp the Pearl, by whatever the wrench.

"He was hunger-bitten, I heard: I tempted with half my store,
And a gibe was all my thanks. Is he generous like Spring dew?
Account the fault to me who chaffered with such an one!
He has killed, to feast chance comers, the creature he rode: nay, more—
For a couple of singing-girls his robe has he torn in two:
I will beg! Yet I nowise gained by the tale of my wife and son.

"I swear by the Holy House, my head will I never wash
Till I filch his Pearl away. Fair dealing I tried, then guile,
And now I resort to force. He said we must live or die:
Let him die, then,—let me live: Be bold—but not too rash!
I have found me a peeping-place: breast, bury your breathing while
I explore for myself! Now, breathe! He deceived me not, the spy!

"As he said—there lies in peace Hóseyn—how happy! Beside
Stands tethered the Pearl: thrice winds her headstall about his wrist:
'T is therefore he sleeps so sound—the moon through the roof reveals.
And, loose on his left, stands too that other, known far and wide,
Buhéyseh, her sister born: fleet is she yet ever missed
The winning tail's fire-flash a-stream past the thunderous heels.

"No less she stands saddled and bridled, this second, in case some thief
Should enter and seize and fly with the first, as I mean to do.
What then? The Pearl is the Pearl: once mount her we both escape."
Through the skirt-fold in glides Duhl,—so a serpent disturbs no leaf
In a bush as he parts the twigs entwining a nest: clean through,
He is noiselessly at his work: as he planned, he performs the rape.

He has set the tent-door wide, has buckled the girth, has clipped
The headstall away from the wrist he leaves thrice bound as before,
He springs on the Pearl, is launched on the desert like bolt from bow.
Up starts our plundered man: from his breast though the heart be ripped,
Yet his mind has the mastery: behold, in a minute more,
He is out and off and away on Buhéyseh, whose worth we know!

And Hóseyn—his blood turns flame, he has learned long since to ride,
And Buhéyseh does her part,—they gain—they are gaining fast
On the fugitive pair, and Duhl has Ed-Dárraj to cross and quit,
And to reach the ridge El-Sabán,—no safety till that be spied!
And Buhéyseh is, bound by bound, but a horse-length off at last,
For the Pearl has missed the tap of the heel, the touch of the bit.

She shortens her stride, she chafes at her rider the strange and queer:
Buhéyseh is mad with hope—beat sister she shall and must,
Though Duhl, of the hand and heel so clumsy, she has to thank.
She is near now, nose by tail—they are neck by croup—joy! fear!
What folly makes Hóseyn shout "Dog Duhl, Damned son of the Dust,
Touch the right ear and press with your foot my Pearl's left flank!"

And Duhl was wise at the word, and Muléykeh as prompt perceived
Who was urging redoubled pace, and to hear him was to obey,
And a leap indeed gave she, and evanished forevermore.
And Hóseyn looked one long last look as who, all bereaved,
Looks, fain to follow the dead so far as the living may:
Then he turned Buhéyseh's neck slow homeward, weeping sore.

And, lo, in the sunrise, still sat Hóseyn upon the ground
Weeping: and neighbors came, the tribesmen of Bénu-Asád
In the vale of green Er-Rass, and they questioned him of his grief;
And he told from first to last how, serpent-like, Duhl had wound
His way to the nest, and how Duhl rode like an ape, so bad!
And how Buhéyseh did wonders, yet Pearl remained with the thief.

And they jeered him, one and all: "Poor Hóseyn is crazed past hope!
How else had he wrought himself his ruin, in fortune's spite?
To have simply held the tongue were a task for boy or girl,
And here were Muléykeh again, the eyed like an antelope,
The child of his heart by day, the wife of his breast by night!"—
"And the beaten in speed!" wept Hóseyn. "You never have loved my
Pearl."

PIETRO OF ABANO

Petrus Aponensis—there was a magician!
When that strange adventure happened, which I mean to tell my hearers,
Nearly had he tried all trades—beside physician,
Architect, astronomer, astrologer,—or worse:
How else, as the old books warrant, was he able,
All at once, through all the world, to prove the promptest of appearers
Where was prince to cure, tower to build as high as Babel,
Star to name or sky-sign read,—yet pouch, for pains, a curse?

—Curse: for when a vagrant,—foot-sore, travel-tattered,
Now a young man, now an old man, Turk or Arab, Jew or Gypsy,—
Proffered folk in passing—Oh, for pay, what mattered?—
"I 'll be doctor, I 'll play builder, star I 'll name—sign read!"
Soon as prince was cured, tower built, and fate predicted,
"Who may you be?" came the question; when he answered "Petrus ipse,"
"Just as we divined!" cried folk—"A wretch convicted
Long ago of dealing with the devil—-you indeed!"

So, they cursed him roundly, all his labor's payment,
Motioned him—the convalescent prince would—to vacate the presence:
Babylonians plucked his beard and tore his raiment,
Drove him from that tower he built: while, had he peered at stars,
Town howled "Stone the quack who styles our Dog-star—Sirius!"
Country yelled "Aroint the churl who prophesies we take no pleasance
Under vine and fig-tree, since the year 's delirious,
Bears no crop of any kind,—all through the planet Mars!"

Straightway would the whilom youngster grow a grisard,

Or, as case might hap, the hoary eld drop off" and show a stripling.
Town and country groaned—indebted to a wizard!
"Curse—nay, kick and cuff him—fit requital of his pains!
Gratitude in word or deed were wasted truly!
Rather make the Church amends by crying out on, cramping, crippling
One who, on pretence of serving man, serves duly
Man's arch foe: not ours, be sure, but Satan's—his the gains!"

Peter grinned and bore it, such disgraceful usage:
Somehow, cuffs and kicks and curses seem ordained his like to suffer:
Prophet's pay with Christians, now as in the Jews' age,
Still is—stoning: so, he meekly took his wage and went,
—Safe again was found ensconced in those old quarters,
Padua's blackest blindest by-street,—none the worse, nay, somewhat tougher:
"Calculating," quoth he, "soon I join the martyrs,
Since, who magnify my lore on burning me are bent."

Therefore, on a certain evening, to his alley
Peter slunk, all bruised and broken, sore in body, sick in spirit,
Just escaped from Cairo where he launched a galley
Needing neither sails nor oars nor help of wind or tide,
—Needing but the fume of fire to set a-flying
Wheels like mad which whirled you quick—North, South, where'er you pleased require it,—
That is—would have done so had not priests come prying,
Broke his engine up and bastinadoed him beside.

As he reached his lodging, stopped there unmolested,
(Neighbors feared him, urchins fled him, few were bold enough to follow)
While his fumbling fingers tried the lock and tested
Once again the queer key's virtue, oped the sullen door,—
Some one plucked his sleeve, cried, "Master, pray your pardon!
Grant a word to me who patient wait you in your archway's hollow!
Hard on you men's hearts are: be not your heart hard on
Me who kiss your garment's hem, O Lord of magic lore!

"Mage—say I, who no less, scorning tittle-tattle,
To the vulgar give no credence when they prate of Peter's magic,
Deem his art brews tempest, hurts the crops and cattle,
Hinders fowls from laying eggs and worms from spinning silk,
Rides upon a he-goat, mounts at need a broomstick:
While the price he pays for this (so turns to comic what was tragic)
Is—he may not drink—dreads like the Day of Doom's tick—
One poor drop of sustenance ordained mere men—that 's milk!

"Tell such tales to Padua! Think me no such dullard!
Not from these benighted parts did I derive my breath and being!
I am from a land whose cloudless skies are colored
Livelier, suns orb largelier, airs seem incense,—while, on earth—

What, instead of grass, our fingers and our thumbs cull,
Proves true moly! sounds and sights there help the body's hearing, seeing,
Till the soul grows godlike: brief,—you front no numskull
Shaming by ineptitude the Greece that gave him birth!

"Mark within my eye its iris mystic-lettered—
That 's my name! and note my ear—its swan-shaped cavity, my emblem!
Mine 's the swan-like nature born to fly unfettered
Over land and sea in search of knowledge—food for song.
Art denied the vulgar! Geese grow fat on barley,
Swans require ethereal provend, undesirous to resemble 'em—
Soar to seek Apollo—favored with a parley
Such as, Master, you grant me—who will not hold you long.

"Leave to learn to sing—for that your swan petitions:
Master, who possess the secret, say not nay to such a suitor!
All I ask is—bless mine, purest of ambitions!
Grant me leave to make my kind wise, free, and happy! How?
Just by making me—as you are mine—their model!
Geese have goose-thoughts: make a swan their teacher first, then coadjutor,—
Let him introduce swan-notions to each noddle,—
Geese will soon grow swans, and men become what I am now!

"That 's the only magic—had but fools discernment,
Could they probe and pass into the solid through the soft and seeming!
Teach me such true magic—now, and no adjournment!
Teach your art of making fools subserve the man of mind!
Magic is the power we men of mind should practice,
Draw fools to become our drudges—docile henceforth, never dreaming—
While they do our hests for fancied gain—the fact is
What they toil and moil to get proves falsehood: truth 's behind!

"See now! you conceive some fabric—say, a mansion
Meet for monarch's pride and pleasure: this is truth—a thought has fired you,
Made you fain to give some cramped concept expansion,
Put your faculty to proof, fulfil your nature's task.
First you fascinate the monarch's self: he fancies
He it was devised the scheme you execute as he inspired you:
He in turn sets slaving insignificances
Toiling, moiling till your structure stands there—all you ask!

"Soon the monarch 's known for what he was—a ninny:
Soon the rabble-rout leave labor, take their work-day wage and vanish:
Soon the late puffed bladder, pricked, shows lank and skinny—
'Who was its inflator?' ask we, 'whose the giant lungs'
Petri en pulmones! What though men prove ingrates?
Let them—so they stop at crucifixion—buffet, ban and banish!
Peter's power's apparent: human praise—its din grates

Harsh as blame on ear unused to aught save angels' tongues.

"Ay, there have been always, since our world existed,
Mages who possessed the secret—needed but to stand still, fix eye
On the foolish mortal: straight was he enlisted
Soldier, scholar, servant, slave—no matter for the style!
Only through illusion; ever what seemed profit—
Love or lucre—justified obedience to the Ipse dixi:
Work done—palace reared from pavement up to soffit—
Was it strange if builders smelt out cheating all the while?

"Let them pelt and pound, bruise, bray you in a mortar!
What 's the odds to you who seek reward of quite another nature?
You 've enrolled your name where sages of your sort are,
—Michael of Constantinople, Hans of Halberstadt!
Nay and were you nameless, still you 've your conviction
You it was and only you—what signifies the nomenclature?—
Ruled the world in fact, though how you ruled be fiction
Fit for fools: true wisdom's magic you—if e'er man—had 't!

"But perhaps you ask me, 'Since each ignoramus
While he profits by such magic persecutes the benefactor,
What should I expect but—once I render famous
You as Michael, Hans, and Peter—just one ingrate more?
If the vulgar prove thus, whatsoe'er the pelf be,
Pouched through my beneficence—and doom me dungeoned, chained, or racked, or
Fairly burned outright—how grateful will yourself be
When, his secret gained, you match your—master just before?'

"That 's where I await you! Please, revert a little!
What do folk report about you if not this—which, though chimeric,
Still, as figurative, suits you to a tittle—
That,—although the elements obey your nod and wink,
Fades or flowers the herb you chance to smile or sigh at,
While your frown bids earth quake palled by obscuration atmospheric,—
Brief, although through nature naught resists your fiat,
There 's yet one poor substance mocks you—milk you may not drink!

"Figurative language! Take my explanation!
Fame with fear, and hate with homage, these your art procures in plenty.
All 's but daily dry bread: what makes moist the ration?
Love, the milk that sweetens man his meal—alas, you lack:
I am he who, since he fears you not, can love you.
Love is born of heart not mind, de corde natus haud de mente;
Touch my heart and love 's yours, sure as shines above you
Sun by day and star by night though earth should go to wrack!

"Stage by stage you lift me—kiss by kiss I hallow

Whose but your dear hand my helper, punctual as at each new impulse
I approach my aim? Shell chipped, the eaglet callow
Needs a parent's pinion-push to quit the eyrie's edge:
But once fairly launched forth, denizen of ether,
While each effort sunward bids the blood more freely through each limb pulse,
Sure the parent feels, as gay they soar together,
Fully are all pains repaid when love redeems its pledge!"

Then did Peter's tristful visage lighten somewhat,
Vent a watery smile as though inveterate mistrust were thawing.
"Well, who knows?" he slow broke silence. "Mortals—come what
Come there may—are still the dupes of hope there 's luck in store.
Many scholars seek me, promise mounts and marvels:
Here stand I to witness how they step 'twixt me and clapper-clawing!
Dry bread,—that I 've gained me: truly I should starve else:
But of milk, no drop was mine! Well, shuffle cards once more!"

At the word of promise thus implied, our stranger—
What can he but cast his arms, in rapture of embrace, round Peter?
"Hold! I choke!" the mage grunts. "Shall I in the manger
Any longer play the dog? Approach, my calf, and feed!
Bene ... won't you wait for grace?" But sudden incense
Wool-white, serpent-solid, curled up—perfume growing sweet and sweeter
Till it reached the young man's nose and seemed to win sense
Soul and all from out his brain through nostril: yes, indeed!

Presently the young man rubbed his eyes. "Where am I?
Too much bother over books! Some reverie has proved amusing.
What did Peter prate of? 'Faith, my brow is clammy!
How my head throbs, how my heart thumps! Can it be I swooned?
Oh, I spoke my speech out—cribbed from Plato's tractate,
Dosed him with 'the Fair and Good,' swore—Dog of Egypt—I was choosing
Plato's way to serve men! What 's the hour? Exact eight!
Home now, and to-morrow never mind how Plato mooned!

"Peter has the secret! Fair and Good are products
(So he said) of Foul and Evil: one must bring to pass the other.
Just as poisons grow drugs, steal through sundry odd ducts
Doctors name, and ultimately issue safe and changed.
You 'd abolish poisons, treat disease with dainties
Such as suit the sound and sane? With all such kickshaws vain you pother!
Arsenic 's the stuff puts force into the faint eyes,
Opium sets the brain to rights—by cark and care deranged.

"What, he 's safe within door?—would escape—no question—
Thanks, since thanks and more I owe, and mean to pay in time befitting.
What most presses now is—after night's digestion,
Peter, of thy precepts!—promptest practice of the same.

Let me see! The wise man, first of all, scorns riches:
But to scorn them must obtain them: none believes in his permitting
Gold to lie ungathered: who picks up, then pitches
Gold away—philosophizes: none disputes his claim.

"So with worldly honors: 't is by abdicating,
Incontestably he proves he could have kept the crown discarded.
Sulla cuts a figure, leaving off dictating:
Simpletons laud private life? 'The grapes are sour,' laugh we.
So, again—but why continue? All 's tumultuous
Here: my head 's a-whirl with knowledge. Speedily shall be rewarded
He who taught me! Greeks prove ingrates? So insult you us?
When your teaching bears its first-fruits, Peter—wait and see!"

As the word, the deed proved; ere a brief year's passage,
Fop—that fool he made the jokes on—now he made the jokes for, gratis:
Hunks—that hoarder, long left lonely in his crass age—
Found now one appreciative deferential friend:
Powder-paint-and-patch, Hag Jezebel—recovered,
Strange to say, the power to please, got courtship till she cried Jam satis!
Fop be-flattered. Hunks be-friended, Hag be-lovered—
Nobody o'erlooked, save God—he soon attained his end.

As he lounged at ease one morning in his villa,
(Hag's the dowry) estimated (Hunks' bequest) his coin in coffer,
Mused on how a fool's good word (Fop's word) could fill a
Social circle with his praise, promote him man of mark,—
All at once—"An old friend fain would see your Highness!"
There stood Peter, skeleton and scarecrow, plain writ Phi-lo-so-pher
In the woe-worn face—for yellowness and dryness,
Parchment—with, a pair of eyes—one hope their feeble spark.

"Did I counsel rightly? Have you, in accordance,
Prospered greatly, dear my pupil? Sure, at just the stage I find you,
When your hand may draw me forth from the mad war-dance
Savages are leading round your master—down, not dead.
Padua wants to burn me: balk them, let me linger
Life out—rueful though its remnant—hid in some safe hold behind you!
Prostrate here I lie: quick, help with but a finger
Lest I house in safety's self—a tombstone o'er my head!

"Lodging, bite and sup, with—now and then—a copper
—Alms for any poorer still, if such there be,—is all my asking.
Take me for your bedesman,—nay, if you think proper,
Menial merely,—such my perfect passion for repose!
Yes, from out your plenty Peter craves a pittance
—Leave to thaw his frozen hands before the fire whereat you 're basking!
Double though your debt were, grant this boon—remittance

He proclaims of obligation: 't is himself that owes!"

"Venerated Master—can it be, such treatment
Learning meets with, magic fails to guard you from, by all appearance?
Strange! for, as you entered,—what the famous feat meant,
I was full of,—why you reared that fabric, Padua's boast.
Nowise for man's pride, man's pleasure, did you slyly
Raise it, but man's seat of rule whereby the world should soon have clearance
(Happy world) from such a rout as now so vilely
Handles you—and hampers me, for which I grieve the most.

"Since if it got wind you now were my familiar,
How could I protect you—nay, defend myself against the rabble?
Wait until the mob, now masters, willy-nilly are
Servants as they should be: then has gratitude full play!
Surely this experience shows how unbefitting
'T is that minds like mine should rot in ease and plenty. Geese may gabble,
Gorge, and keep the ground: but swans are soon for quitting
Earthly fare—as fain would I, your swan, if taught the way.

"Teach me, then, to rule men, have them at my pleasure!
Solely for their good, of course,—impart a secret worth rewarding,
Since the proper life's—prize! Tantalus's treasure
Aught beside proves, vanishes, and leaves no trace at all.
Wait awhile, nor press for payment prematurely!
Over-haste defrauds you. Thanks! since,—even while I speak,—discarding
Sloth and vain delights, I learn how—swiftly, surely—
Magic sways the sceptre, wears the crown and wields the ball!

"Gone again—what, is he? 'Faith, he 's soon disposed of!
Peter's precepts work already, put within my lump their leaven!
Ay, we needs must don glove would we pluck the rose—doff
Silken garment would we climb the tree and take its fruit.
Why sharp thorn, rough rind? To keep unviolated
Either prize! We garland us, we mount from earth to feast in heaven,
Just because exist what once we estimated
Hindrances which, better taught, as helps we now compute.

"Foolishly I turned disgusted from my fellows!
Pits of ignorance—to fill, and heaps of prejudice—to level—
Multitudes in motley, whites and blacks and yellows—
What a hopeless task it seemed to discipline the host!
Now I see my error. Vices act like virtues
—Not alone because they guard—sharp thorns—the rose we first dishevel,
Not because they scrape, scratch—rough rind—through the dirt-shoes
Bare feet cling to bole with, while the half-mooned boot we boast.

"No, my aim is nobler, more disinterested!

Man shall keep what seemed to thwart him, since it proves his true assistance,
Leads to ascertaining which head is the best head,
Would he crown his body, rule its members—lawless else.
Ignorant the horse stares, by deficient vision
Takes a man to be a monster, lets him mount, then, twice the distance
Horse could trot unridden, gallops—dream Elysian!—
Dreaming that his dwarfish guide's a giant,—jockeys tell 's."

Brief, so worked the spell, he promptly had a riddance:
Heart and brain no longer felt the pricks which passed for conscience-scruples:
Free henceforth his feet,—Per Bacco, how they did dance
Merrily through lets and checks that stopped the way before!
Politics the prize now,—such adroit adviser.
Opportune suggester, with the tact that triples and quadruples
Merit in each measure,—never did the Kaiser
Boast as subject such a statesman, friend, and something more!

As he, up and down, one noonday, paced his closet
—Council o'er, each spark (his hint) blown flame, by colleagues' breath applauded,
Strokes of statecraft hailed with "Salomo si nôsset!"
(His the nostrum)—every throw for luck come double-six,—
As he, pacing, hugged himself in satisfaction,
Thump—the door went. "What, the Kaiser? By none else were I defrauded
Thus of well-earned solace. Since 't is fate's exaction,—
Enter, Liege my Lord! Ha, Peter, you here? Teneor vix!"

"Ah, Sir, none the less, contain you, nor wax irate!
You so lofty, I so lowly,—vast the space which yawns between us!
Still, methinks, you—more than ever—at a high rate
Needs must prize poor Peter's secret since it lifts you thus.
Grant me now the boon whereat before you boggled!
Ten long years your march has moved—one triumph—(though e 's short)—hactēnus,
While I down and down disastrously have joggled
Till I pitch against Death's door, the true Nec Ultra Plus.

"Years ago—some ten 't is—since I sought for shelter,
Craved in your whole house a closet, out of all your means a comfort.
Now you soar above these: as is gold to spelter
So is power—you urged with reason—paramount to wealth.
Power you boast in plenty: let it grant me refuge!
House-room now is out of question: find for me some stronghold—some fort—
Privacy wherein, immured, shall this blind deaf huge
Monster of a mob let stay the soul I 'd save by stealth!

"Ay, for all too much with magic have I tampered!
—Lost the world, and gained, I fear, a certain place I 'm to describe loth!
Still, if prayer and fasting tame the pride long pampered,
Mercy may be mine: amendment never comes too late.

How can I amend beset by cursers, kickers?
Pluck this brand from out the burning! Once away, I take my Bible-oath,
Never more—so long as life's weak lamp-flame flickers—
No, not once I 'll tease you, but in silence bear my fate!"

"Gently, good my Genius, Oracle unerring!
Strange now! can you guess on what—as in you peeped—it was I pondered?
You and I are both of one mind in preferring
Power to wealth, but—here 's the point—what sort of power, I ask?
Ruling men is vulgar, easy, and ignoble:
Rid yourself of conscience, quick you have at beck and call the fond herd.
But who wields the crozier, down may fling the crow-bill:
That 's the power I covet now; soul's sway o'er souls—my task!

"'Well but,' you object, 'you have it, who by glamour
Dress up lies to look like truths, mask folly in the garb of reason:
Your soul acts on theirs, sure, when the people clamour,
Hold their peace, now fight now fondle,—earwigged through the brains.'
Possibly! but still the operation 's mundane,
Grosser than a taste demands which—craving manna—kecks at peason—
Power o'er men by wants material: why should one deign
Rule by sordid hopes and fears—a grunt for all one's pains?

"No, if men must praise me, let them praise to purpose!
Would we move the world, not earth but heaven must be our fulcrum—pou sto!
Thus I seek to move it: Master, why intérpose—
Balk my climbing close on what 's the ladder's topmost round?
Statecraft 't is I step from: when by priestcraft hoisted
Up to where my foot may touch the highest rung which fate allows toe,
Then indeed ask favor. On you shall be foisted
No excuse: I 'll pay my debt, each penny of the pound!

"Ho, my knaves without there! Lead this worthy downstairs!
No farewell, good Paul—nay, Peter—what 's your name remembered rightly?
Come, he 's humble: out another would have flounced—airs
Suitors often give themselves when our sort bow them forth.
Did I touch his rags? He surely kept his distance:
Yet, there somehow passed to me from him—where'er the virtue might lie—
Something that inspires my soul—Oh, by assistance
Doubtlessly of Peter!—still, he 's worth just what he 's worth!

"'T is my own soul soars now: soaring—how? By crawling!
I 'll to Rome, before Rome's feet the temporal-supreme lay prostrate!
'Hands' (I 'll say) 'proficient once in pulling, hauling
This and that way men as I was minded—feet now clasp!'
Ay, the Kaiser's self has wrung them in his fervor!
Now—they only sue to slave for Rome, nor at one doit the cost rate.
Rome's adopted child—no bone, no muscle, nerve or

Sinew of me but I 'll strain, though out my life I gasp!"

As he stood one evening proudly—(he had traversed
Rome on horseback—peerless pageant!—claimed the Lateran as new Pope)—
Thinking "All 's attained now! Pontiff! Who could have erst
Dreamed of my advance so far when, some ten years ago,
I embraced devotion, grew from priest to bishop,
Gained the Purple, bribed the Conclave, got the Two-thirds, saw my coop ope,
Came out—what Rome hails me! O were there a wish-shop,
Not one wish more would I purchase—lord of all below!

"Ha—who dares intrude now—puts aside the arras?
What, old Peter, here again, at such a time, in such a presence?
Satan sends this plague back merely to embarrass
Me who enter on my office—little needing you!
'Faith, I 'm touched myself by age, but you look Tithon!
Were it vain to seek of you the sole prize left—rejuvenescence?
Well, since flesh is grass which time must lay his scythe on,
Say your say and so depart and make no more ado!"

Peter faltered—coughing first by way of prologue—
"Holiness, your help comes late: a death at ninety little matters.
Padua, build poor Peter's pyre now, on log roll log,
Burn away—I 've lived my day! Yet here 's the sting in death—
I 've an author's pride: I want my Book's survival:
See, I 've hid it in my breast to warm me 'mid the rags and tatters!
Save it—tell next age your Master had no rival!
Scholar's debt discharged in full, be 'Thanks' my latest breath!"

"Faugh, the frowsy bundle—scribblings harum-scarum
Scattered o'er a dozen sheepskins! What 's the name of this farrago?
Ha—'Conciliator Differentiarum'—
Man and book may burn together, cause the world no loss!
Stop—what else? A tractate—eh, 'De Speciebus
Ceremonialis Ma-gi-æ?' I dream sure! Hence, away, go,
Wizard,—quick avoid me! Vain you clasp my knee, buss
Hand that bears the Fisher's ring or foot that boasts the Cross!

"Help! The old magician clings like an octopus!
Ah, you rise now—fuming, fretting, frowning, if I read your features!
Frown, who cares? We 're Pope—once Pope, you can't unpope us!
Good—you muster up a smile: that 's better! Still so brisk?
All at once grown youthful? But the case is plain! Ass—
Here I dally with the fiend, yet know the Word—compels all creatures
Earthly, heavenly, hellish. Apage, Sathanas
Dicam verbum Salomonis—" "dicite!" When—whisk!—

What was changed? The stranger gave his eyes a rubbing:

There smiled Peter's face turned back a moment at him o'er the shoulder,
As the black-door shut, bang! "So he 'scapes a drubbing!"
(Quoth a boy who, unespied, had stopped to hear the talk.)
"That 's the way to thank these wizards when they bid men
Benedicite! What ails you? You, a man, and yet no bolder?
Foreign Sir, you look but foolish!" "Idmen, idmen!"
Groaned the Greek. "O Peter, cheese at last I know from chalk!"

Peter lived his life out, menaced yet no martyr,
Knew himself the mighty man he was—such knowledge all his guerdon,
Left the world a big book—people but in part err
When they style a true Scientiæ Com-pen-di-um:
"Admirationem incutit" they sourly
Smile, as fast they shut the folio which myself was somehow spurred on
Once to ope: but love—life's milk which daily, hourly,
Blockheads lap—O Peter, still thy taste of love 's to come!

Greek, was your ambition likewise doomed to failure?
True, I find no record you wore purple, walked with axe and fasces,
Played some antipope's part: still, friend, don't turn tail, you 're
Certain, with but these two gifts, to gain earth's prize in time!
Cleverness uncurbed by conscience—if you ransacked
Peter's book you 'd find no potent spell like these to rule the masses;
Nor should want example, had I not to transact
Other business. Go your ways, you 'll thrive! So ends my rhyme.

When these parts Tiberius—not yet Cæsar—travelled,
Passing Padua, he consulted Padua's Oracle of Geryon
(God three-headed, thrice wise) just to get unravelled
Certain tangles of his future. "Fling at Abano
Golden dice," it answered: "dropt within the fount there,
Note what sum the pips present!" And still we see each die, the very one,
Turn up, through the crystal,—read the whole account there
Where 't is told by Suetonius,—each its highest throw.

Scarce the sportive fancy-dice I fling show "Venus:"
Still—for love of that dear land which I so oft in dreams revisit—
I have—oh, not sung! but lilted (as—between us—
Grows my lazy custom) this its legend. What the lilt?

[Music]

DOCTOR ——

A Rabbi told me: On the day allowed
Satan for carping at God's rule, he came,

Fresh from our earth, to brave the angel-crowd.

"What is the fault now?" "This I find to blame:
Many and various are the tongues below,
Yet all agree in one speech, all proclaim

"'Hell has no might to match what earth, can show:
Death is the strongest-born of Hell, and yet
Stronger than Death is a Bad Wife, we know.'

"Is it a wonder if I fume and fret—
Robbed of my rights, since Death am I, and mine
The style of Strongest? Men pay Nature's debt

"Because they must at my demand; decline
To pay it henceforth surely men will please,
Provided husbands with bad wives combine

"To baffle Death. Judge between me and these!"
"Thyself shalt judge. Descend to earth in shape
Of mortal, marry, drain from froth to lees

"The bitter draught, then see if thou escape
Concluding, with men sorrowful and sage,
A Bad Wife's strength Death's self in vain would ape!"

How Satan entered on his pilgrimage,
Conformed himself to earthly ordinance,
Wived and played husband well from youth to age

Intrepidly—I leave untold, advance
Through many a married year until I reach
A day when—of his father's countenance

The very image, like him too in speech
As well as thought and deed,—the union's fruit
Attained maturity. "I needs must teach

"My son a trade: but trade, such son to suit,
Needs seeking after. He a man of war?
Too cowardly! A lawyer wins repute—

"Having to toil and moil, though—both which are
Beyond this sluggard. There 's Divinity:
No, that 's my own bread-winner—that be far

"From my poor offspring! Physic? Ha, we 'll try
If this be practicable. Where 's my wit?

Asleep?—since, now I come to think ... Ay, ay!

"Hither, my son! Exactly have I hit
On a profession for thee. Medicus—
Behold, thou art appointed! Yea, I spit

"Upon thine eyes, bestow a virtue thus
That henceforth not this human form I wear
Shalt thou perceive alone, but—one of us

"By privilege—thy fleshly sight shall bear
Me in my spirit-person as I walk
The world and take my prey appointed there.

"Doctor once dubbed—what ignorance shall balk
Thy march triumphant? Diagnose the gout
As colic, and prescribe it cheese for chalk—

"No matter! All 's one: cure shall come about
And win thee wealth—fees paid with such a roar
Of thanks and praise alike from lord and lout

"As never stunned man's ears on earth before.
'How may this be?' Why, that 's my skeptic! Soon
Truth will corrupt thee, soon thou doubt'st no more!

"Why is it I bestow on thee the boon
Of recognizing me the while I go
Invisibly among men, morning, noon,

"And night, from house to house, and—quick or slow—
Take my appointed prey? They summon thee
For help, suppose: obey the summons! so!

"Enter, look round! Where 's Death? Know—I am he,
Satan who work all evil: I who bring
Pain to the patient in whate'er degree.

"I, then, am there: first glance thine eye shall fling
Will find me—whether distant or at hand,
As I am free to do my spiriting.

"At such mere first glance thou shalt understand
Wherefore I reach no higher up the room
Than door or window, when my form is scanned.

"Howe'er friends' faces please to gather gloom,
Bent o'er the sick,—howe'er himself desponds,—

In such case Death is not the sufferer's doom.

"Contrariwise, do friends rejoice my bonds
Are broken, does the captive in his turn
Crow 'Life shall conquer'? Nip these foolish fronds

"Of hope a-sprout, if haply thou discern
Me at the head—my victim's head, be sure!
Forth now! This taught thee, little else to learn!"

And forth he went. Folk heard him ask demure,
"How do you style this ailment? (There he peeps,
My father through the arras!) Sirs, the cure

"Is plain as A B C! Experience steeps
Blossoms of pennyroyal half an hour
In sherris. Sumat!—Lo, how sound he sleeps—

"The subject you presumed was past the power
Of Galen to relieve!" Or else, "How 's this?
Why call for help so tardily? Clouds lour

"Portentously indeed, Sirs! (Naught 's amiss:
He 's at the bed-foot merely.) Still, the storm
May pass averted—not by quacks, I wis,

"Like you, my masters! You, forsooth, perform
A miracle? Stand, sciolists, aside!
Blood, ne'er so cold, at ignorance grows warm!"

Which boasting by result was justified,
Big as might words be: whether drugged or left
Drugless, the patient always lived, not died.

Great the heir's gratitude, so nigh bereft
Of all he prized in this world: sweet the smile
Of disconcerted rivals: "Cure?—say, theft

"From Nature in despite of Art—so style
This off-hand kill-or-cure work! You did much,
I had done more: folk cannot wait awhile!"

But did the case change? was it—"Scarcely such
The symptoms as to warrant our recourse
To your skill, Doctor! Yet since just a touch

"Of pulse, a taste of breath, has all the force
With you of long investigation claimed

By others,—tracks an ailment to its source

"Intuitively,—may we ask unblamed
What from this pimple you prognosticate?"
"Death!" was the answer, as he saw and named

The coucher by the sick man's head. "Too late
You send for my assistance. I am bold
Only by Nature's leave, and bow to Fate!

"Besides, you have my rivals: lavish gold!
How comfortably quick shall life depart
Cosseted by attentions manifold!

"One day, one hour ago, perchance my art
Had done some service. Since you have yourselves
Chosen—before the horse—to put the cart,

"Why, Sirs, the sooner that the sexton delves
Your patient's grave the better! How you stare
—Shallow, for all the deep books on your shelves!

"Fare you well, fumblers!" Do I need declare
What name and fame, what riches recompensed
The Doctor's practice? Never anywhere

Such an adept as daily evidenced
Each new vaticination! Oh, not he
Like dolts who dallied with their scruples, fenced

With subterfuge, nor gave out frank and free
Something decisive! If he said "I save
The patient," saved he was: if "Death will be

"His portion," you might count him dead. Thus brave,
Behold our worthy, sans competitor
Throughout the country, on the architrave

Of Glory's temple golden-lettered for
Machaon redivivus! So, it fell
That, of a sudden, when the Emperor

Was smit by sore disease, I need not tell
If any other Doctor's aid was sought
To come and forthwith make the sick Prince well.

"He will reward thee as a monarch ought.
Not much imports the malady; but then,

He clings to life and cries like one distraught

"For thee—who, from a simple citizen,
Mayst look to rise in rank,—nay, haply wear
A medal with his portrait,—always when

"Recovery is quite accomplished. There!
Pass to the presence!" Hardly has he crossed
The chamber's threshold when he halts, aware

Of who stands sentry by the head. All 's lost.
"Sire, naught avails my art: you near the goal,
And end the race by giving up the ghost."

"How?" cried the monarch: "Names upon your roll
Of half my subjects rescued by your skill—
Old and young, rich and poor—crowd cheek by jowl

"And yet no room for mine? Be saved I will!
Why else am I earth's foremost potentate?
Add me to these and take as fee your fill

"Of gold—that point admits of no debate
Between us: save me, as you can and must,—
Gold, till your gown's pouch cracks beneath the weight!"

This touched the Doctor. "Truly a home-thrust,
Parent, you will not parry! Have I dared
Entreat that you forego the meal of dust

"—Man that is snake's meat—when I saw prepared
Your daily portion? Never! Just this once,
Go from his head, then,—let his life be spared!"

Whisper met whisper in the gruff response;
"Fool, I must have my prey: no inch I budge
From where thou see'st me thus myself ensconce."

"Ah," moaned the sufferer, "by thy look I judge
Wealth fails to tempt thee: what if honors prove
More efficacious? Naught to him I grudge

"Who saves me. Only keep my head above
The cloud that 's creeping round it—I 'll divide
My empire with thee! No? What 's left but—love?

"Does love allure thee? Well then, take as bride
My only daughter, fair beyond belief!

Save me—to-morrow shall the knot be tied!"

"Father, you hear him! Respite ne'er so brief
Is all I beg: go now and come again
Next day, for aught I care: respect the grief

"Mine will be if thy first-born sues in vain!"
"Fool, I must have my prey!" was all he got
In answer. But a fancy crossed his brain.

"I have it! Sire, methinks a meteor shot
Just now across the heavens and neutralized
Jove's salutary influence: 'neath the blot

"Plumb are you placed now: well that I surmised
The cause of failure! Knaves, reverse the bed!"
"Stay!" groaned the monarch, "I shall be capsized—

"Jolt—jolt—my heels uplift where late my head
Was lying—sure I 'm turned right round at last!
What do you say now, Doctor?" Naught he said,

For why? With one brisk leap the Antic passed
From couch-foot back to pillow,—as before,
Lord of the situation. Long aghast

The Doctor gazed, then "Yet one trial more
Is left me" inwardly he uttered. "Shame
Upon thy flinty heart! Do I implore

"This trifling favor in the idle name
Of mercy to the moribund? I plead
The cause of all thou dost affect: my aim

"Befits my author! Why would I succeed?
Simply that by success I may promote
The growth of thy pet virtues—pride and greed.

"But keep thy favors!—curse thee! I devote
Henceforth my service to the other side.
No time to lose: the rattle 's in his throat.

"So,—not to leave one last resource untried,—
Run to my house with all haste, somebody!
Bring me that knobstick thence, so often plied

"With profit by the astrologer—shall I
Disdain its help, the mystic Jacob's-Staff?

Sire, do but have the courage not to die

"Till this arrive! Let none of you dare laugh!
Though rugged its exterior, I have seen
That implement work wonders, send the chaff

"Quick and thick flying from the wheat—I mean,
By metaphor, a human sheaf it threshed
Flail-like. Go fetch it! Or—a word between

Just you and me, friend!—go bid, unabashed,
My mother, whom you 'll find there, bring the stick
Herself—herself, mind!" Out the lackey dashed

Zealous upon the errand. Craft and trick
Are meat and drink to Satan: and he grinned
—How else?—at an excuse so politic

For failure: scarce would Jacob's-Staff rescind
Fate's firm decree! And ever as he neared
The agonizing one, his breath like wind

Froze to the marrow, while his eye-flash seared
Sense in the brain up: closelier and more close
Pressing his prey, when at the door appeared

—Who but his Wife the Bad? Whereof one dose,
One grain, one mite of the medicament,
Sufficed him. Up he sprang. One word, too gross

To soil my lips with,—and through ceiling went
Somehow the Husband. "That a storm 's dispersed
We know for certain by the sulphury scent!

"Hail to the Doctor! Who but one so versed
In all Dame Nature's secrets had prescribed
The staff thus opportunely? Style him first

"And foremost of physicians!" "I've imbibed
Elixir surely," smiled the prince,—"have gained
New lease of life. Dear Doctor, how you bribed

"Death to forego me, boots not: you 've obtained
My daughter and her dowry. Death, I 've heard,
Was still on earth the strongest power that reigned,

"Except a Bad Wife!" Whereunto demurred
Nowise the Doctor, so refused the fee

—No dowry, no bad wife!

"You think absurd
This tale?"—the Rabbi added: "True, our Talmud
Boasts sundry such: yet—have our elders erred
In thinking there 's some water there, not all mud?"
I tell it, as the Rabbi told it me.

PAN AND LUNA

Si credere dignum est.—Georgic, III. 390.

Oh, worthy of belief I hold it was,
Virgil, your legend in those strange three lines!
No question, that adventure came to pass
One black night in Arcadia: yes, the pines,
Mountains and valleys mingling made one mass
Of black with void black heaven: the earth's confines,
The sky's embrace,—below, above, around,
All hardened into black without a bound.

Fill up a swart stone chalice to the brim
With fresh-squeezed yet fast-thickening poppy-juice:
See how the sluggish jelly, late a-swim,
Turns marble to the touch of who would loose
The solid smooth, grown jet from rim to rim,
By turning round the bowl! So night can fuse
Earth with her all-comprising sky. No less.
Light, the least spark, shows air and emptiness.

And thus it proved when—diving into space,
Stript of all vapor, from each web of mist
Utterly film-free—entered on her race
The naked Moon, full-orbed antagonist
Of night and dark, night's dowry: peak to base,
Upstarted mountains, and each valley, kissed
To sudden life, lay silver-bright: in air
Flew she revealed, Maid-Moon with limbs all bare.

Still as she fled, each depth—where refuge seemed—
Opening a lone pale chamber, left distinct
Those limbs: 'mid still-retreating blue, she teemed
Herself with whiteness,—virginal, uncinct
By any halo save what finely gleamed
To outline not disguise her: heaven was linked
In one accord with earth to quaff the joy,

Drain beauty to the dregs without alloy.

Whereof she grew aware. What help? When, lo,
A succorable cloud with sleep lay dense:
Some pinetree-top had caught it sailing slow,
And tethered for a prize: in evidence
Captive lay fleece on fleece of piled-up snow
Drowsily patient: flake-heaped how or whence,
The structure of that succorable cloud,
What matter? Shamed she plunged into its shroud.

Orbed—so the woman-figure poets call
Because of rounds on rounds—that apple-shaped
Head which its hair binds close into a ball
Each side the curving ears—that pure undraped
Pout of the sister paps—that ... Once for all,
Say—her consummate circle thus escaped
With its innumerous circlets, sank absorbed,
Safe in the cloud—O naked Moon full-orbed!

But what means this? The downy swathes combine,
Conglobe, the smothery coy-caressing stuff
Curdles about her! Vain each twist and twine
Those lithe limbs try, encroached on by a fluff
Fitting as close as fits the dented spine
Its flexible ivory outside-flesh: enough!
The plumy drifts contract, condense, constringe,
Till she is swallowed by the feathery springe.

As when a pearl slips lost in the thin foam
Churned on a sea-shore, and, o'er-frothed, conceits
Herself safe-housed in Amphitrite's dome,—
If, through the bladdery wave-worked yeast, she meets
What most she loathes and leaps from,—elf from gnome
No gladlier,—finds that safest of retreats
Bubble about a treacherous hand wide ope
To grasp her—(divers who pick pearls so grope)—

So lay this Maid-Moon clasped around and caught
By rough red Pan, the god of all that tract:
He it was schemed the snare thus subtly wrought
With simulated earth-breath,—wool-tufts packed
Into a billowy wrappage. Sheep far-sought
For spotless shearings yield such: take the fact
As learned Virgil gives it,—how the breed
Whitens itself forever: yes, indeed!

If one forefather ram, though pure as chalk

From tinge on fleece, should still display a tongue
Black 'neath the beast's moist palate, prompt men balk
The propagating plague: he gets no young:
They rather slay him,—sell his hide to calk
Ships with, first steeped in pitch,—nor hands are wrung
In sorrow for his fate: protected thus,
The purity we love is gained for us.

So did Girl-Moon, by just her attribute
Of unmatched modesty betrayed, lie trapped,
Bruised to the breast of Pan, half god half brute,
Raked by his bristly boar-sward while he lapped
—Never say, kissed her! that were to pollute
Love's language—which moreover proves unapt
To tell now she recoiled—as who finds thorns
Where she sought flowers—when, feeling, she touched—horns!

Then—does the legend say?—first moon-eclipse
Happened, first swooning-fit which puzzled sore
The early sages? Is that why she dips
Into the dark, a minute and no more,
Only so long as serves her while she rips
The cloud's womb through and, faultless as before,
Pursues her way? No lesson for a maid
Left she, a maid herself thus trapped, betrayed?

Ha, Virgil? Tell the rest, you! "To the deep
Of his domain the wildwood, Pan forthwith
Called her, and so she followed"—in her sleep,
Surely?—"by no means spurning him." The myth
Explain who may! Let all else go, I keep
—As of a ruin just a monolith—
Thus much, one verse of five words, each a boon:
Arcadia, night, a cloud, Pan, and the moon.

The first ten lines that follow were printed as epilogue to the second series of Dramatic Idyls; the second ten were added to them by Browning in the album of a young American girl in Venice, October, 1880. See The Century for November, 1882.

"Touch him ne'er so lightly, into song he broke:
Soil so quick-receptive,—not one feather-seed,
Not one flower-dust fell but straight its fall awoke
Vitalizing virtue: song would song succeed
Sudden as spontaneous—prove a poet-soul!"
Indeed?
Rock's the song-soil rather, surface hard and bare:
Sun and dew their mildness, storm and frost their rage

Vainly both expend,—few flowers awaken there:
Quiet in its cleft broods—what the after-age
Knows and names a pine, a nation's heritage.

Thus I wrote in London, musing on my betters,
Poets dead and gone; and lo, the critics cried,
"Out on such a boast!" as if I dreamed that fetters
Binding Dante bind up—me! as if true pride
Were not also humble!
So I smiled and sighed
As I oped your book in Venice this bright morning,
Sweet new friend of mine! and felt the clay or sand,
Whatsoe'er my soil be, break—for praise or scorning—
Out in grateful fancies—weeds; but weeds expand
Almost into flowers, held by such a kindly hand.

THE BLIND MAN TO THE MAIDEN

Browning translated the following from a German poem in Wilhelmine von Hillern's novel The Hour Will Come at the request of Mrs. Clara Bell, the translator of the novel. It there appeared as the work of an anonymous friend, but was reprinted as Browning's in The Whitehall Review for March 1, 1883.

The blind man to the maiden said,
"O thou of hearts the truest,
Thy countenance is hid from me;
Let not my question anger thee!
Speak, though in words the fewest.

"Tell me, what kind of eyes are thine?
Dark eyes, or light ones rather?"
"My eyes are a decided brown—
So much, at least, by looking down,
From the brook's glass I gather."

"And is it red—thy little month?
That too the blind must care for."
"Ah! I would tell it soon to thee,
Only—none yet has told it me.
I cannot answer, therefore.

"But dost thou ask what heart I have—
There hesitate I never.
In thine own breast 't is borne, and so
'T is thine in weal, and thine in woe,
For life, for death—thine ever!"

GOLDONI

The following sonnet was written by Browning for the album of the Committee of the Goldoni monument, erected in Venice in 1883.

Goldoni—good, gay, sunniest of souls,—
Glassing half Venice in that verse of thine,—
What though it just reflect the shade and shine
Of common life, nor render, as it rolls,
Grandeur and gloom? Sufficient for thy shoals
Was Carnival; Parini's depths enshrine
Secrets unsuited to that opaline
Surface of things which laughs along thy scrolls.
There throng the people: how they come and go,
Lisp the soft language, flaunt the bright garb,—see,—
On Piazza, Calle, under Portico
And over Bridge! Dear king of Comedy,
Be honored! thou that didst love Venice so,
Venice, and we who love her, all love thee!

VENICE, November 27, 1883.

Robert Browning – A Short Biography

He is the equal of any Victorian Poet that could be mentioned. However, Browning continues to be in the shadow of Tennyson, Arnold, Hopkins, Morris and many others.

Robert Browning was born on May 7th, 1812 in Walworth in the parish of Camberwell, London. He was baptized on June 14th, 1812, at Lock's Fields Independent Chapel, York Street, Walworth.

Browning's early years were certainly very interesting. His mother was an excellent pianist and a very devout evangelical Christian. His father, who worked as a clerk at the Bank of England, was also an artist, scholar, antiquarian, and collector of books and pictures. Indeed, he amassed more than 6,000 volumes of rare books including works in Greek, Hebrew, Latin, French, Italian, and Spanish. For the young and curious Browning, it was a wonderful resource, added to which his father was a guiding force in his education.

Many accounts attest that Browning was already proficient at reading and writing by the age of five. He is said to have been a bright but anxious student and to have studied and learnt Latin, Greek, and French by the time he was fourteen. From fourteen to sixteen he was educated at home, tutored in music, drawing, dancing, and horsemanship. Certainly, language and the arts were two areas the young Browning both absorbed and pushed himself towards.

At the age of twelve he wrote a volume of Byronic verse he called Incondita, which his parents attempted to have published. The attempts were unsuccessful and, disappointed, Browning destroyed the work.

In 1825, a cousin gave Browning a collection of Percy Bysshe Shelley's poetry; Browning was so enamored with the poems that he asked for the rest of Shelley's works for his thirteenth birthday. In fact, Browning then went the extra mile, declaring himself to be both a vegetarian and an atheist in honour of his hero.

Intriguingly it seems that the rejection of his first volume didn't dim his appreciation of other poets, but it appears to have stopped him writing any poems between the ages of thirteen and twenty.

In 1828, Browning enrolled at the newly-opened University of London. He was uncomfortable with the experience and he soon left, anxious to read and absorb at his own pace.

His education which, overall is notably rambling and lacks a structure that many of his artistic contemporaries enjoyed, i.e. excellent public schooling and then a degree at Oxford or Cambridge, may present many of his critics with ammunition to criticize, but alternatively his hap-hazard education certainly contributed to many of the references that baffled both critics and his audience, but they tellingly show the breath and scale of what he could turn words too. What others would call obscure references were, to Browning, remarkably obvious.

Browning's early career was very promising. His long poem Pauline (of which only a fragment was ever finished and published) brought him to the attention of the Pre-Raphaelite master Dante Gabriel Rossetti and his difficult Paracelsus (published in 1835) was warmly admired by both Dickens and Wordsworth.

In the 1830s he met the actor William Macready and was encouraged to develop and turn his talents to the stage by writing verse drama. But these plays, including Strafford, which ran for five nights in 1837, and those contained within the Bells and Pomegranates series, were, for the most part, unsuccessful.

During this period Browning began to discover that his real talents lay in taking a single character and allowing that character to discover more about himself by revealing further personal aspects of himself in his speeches; the dramatic monologue. The techniques he developed through this—especially the use of diction, rhythm, and symbol—are regarded as his most important contribution to poetry. They would later influence such major poets of the 20th Century as Ezra Pound, T. S. Eliot, and Robert Frost.

By 1840, with the publication of Sordello, the tide turned somewhat. Many thought he was being deliberately obscure, opaque beyond measure and his poetry for the next decade or so was not eagerly acquired or talked about.

As Browning attempted to rehabilitate his career he began a relationship with Elizabeth Barrett in 1845. He had read her poems and, being totally charmed by their quality, was determined to meet her. The poetess was better known than the younger Browning but suffered from a debilitating illness and was also subject to the harsh behaviour of her over-bearing father. Nevertheless, the new couple were soon inseparable.

Her father, as he did with any of his children that married, disinherited her. Despite this she had some money from her own resources and sensing that the best outcome for both the relationship and her own health was to move abroad the couple did just that. After a private marriage at St Marylebone Parish Church, in September 1846, they journeyed to Europe to honeymoon in Paris.

Their new life now took them to Italy, first to Pisa and a little later to Florence. There they absorbed life and one another.

But in the short term the literary assault on Browning's work did not let up. He was now criticized by such patrician writers as Charles Kingsley for his abandonment of England for foreign lands. Browning could do little to answer these attacks except to compose with his pen and continue with his poetical journey.

The Browning's were well respected, and even famous. Elizabeth health began to improve, she grew stronger and in 1849, at the age of 43, between four miscarriages, she gave birth to a son, Robert Wiedeman Barrett Browning, whom they nicknamed "Penini" or "Pen",

Intriguingly despite his growing reputation and return to form as a poet he was more often than not known as 'Elizabeth Barrett's husband'.

Work flowed from his pen that was to ensure his reputation as one of England's leading poets. When his collection Men and Women was published in 1855 it contained some of his finest lines. It was dedicated to Elizabeth. Life had begun to smile handsome rewards upon the Brownings.

Victorian society was very much taken with all things spiritualist. It was not enough to have command of much of the globe through Empire, they wished to know and explore wherever they could. The spirit world beckoned their interest. Browning dissented from this view believing it was all a hoax and a fraud. Elizabeth, however, was inclined to believe and this caused several disagreements between the couple.

They attended a séance by Daniel Dunglas Home, in July 1855. (Home was a famous and clamored after Scottish physical medium with the reported ability to levitate and speak with the dead). It is said that during this séance a spirit face materialised. Home then claimed it was the face of Browning's son who had died in infancy. Browning seized the 'materialisation' which turned out to be Home's bare foot. Browning had never lost a son in infancy.

After the séance, Browning wrote an angry letter to The Times, in which he said: "the whole display of hands, spirit utterances etc., was a cheat and imposture."

The Browning's time in Italy were immensely rewarding years for both their personal and professional lives. Browning encouraged her to include Sonnets from the Portuguese in her published works, these beautiful poems are undoubtedly one of the highlights of English love poetry.

Elizabeth had become quite politicised during these years. Engrossed in Italian politics (which was continuing to slowly re-unify the country), she issued a small volume of political poems entitled Poems before Congress (1860) most of which were written to express her sympathy with the Italian cause after the earlier outbreak of The Second Italian Independence War in 1859. In England they caused uproar. Conservative magazines such as Blackwood's and the Saturday Review labelled her a fanatic. She dedicated the book to her husband.

But in 1861 tragedy struck.

The couple had spent the winter of 1860–61 in Rome when Elizabeth's health deteriorated again and they returned to Florence in early June. However, these turned out to be her final weeks. Only morphine would now still the pain. She died in Browning's arms on June 29th, 1861. Browning said that she died "smilingly, happily, and with a face like a girl's .... Her last word was .... "Beautiful".

Her burial took place in the nearby Protestant English Cemetery of Florence. The local people were deeply saddened, and shops closed their doors in grief and respect.

Browning and their son were obviously devastated. Unable to bear being in Florence without Elizabeth they soon returned to London to live at 19 Warwick Crescent, Maida Vale.

As he re-integrated himself back into the London literary scene he began to finally receive the proper praise, respect and reputation that his works deserved.

Browning went on to publish Dramatis Personæ (1864), and The Ring and the Book (1868–1869). The latter, based on an "old yellow book" which told of a seventeenth-century Italian murder trial, received wide and generous critical acclaim. Although by now he was in the twilight of a long and prolific career, that had achieved some notable ups and downs, he was respected and indeed renowned for his talents and works.

In 1878, he revisited Italy for the first time since Elizabeth's death. He would return there on several further occasions but never to Florence.

Such was the esteem he was held in that The Browning Society was founded in 1881. Although he had never obtained a degree (something that set him apart from many other Victorian poets) he was now awarded honorary degrees from Oxford University in 1882 and then the University of Edinburgh in 1884.

In 1887, Browning produced the major work of his later years, Parleyings with Certain People of Importance in Their Day. Browning now spoke with his own voice as he engaged in a series of dialogues with long-forgotten figures of literary, artistic, and philosophic history. Unfortunately, both the critics and public were completely baffled by this.

On April 7th, 1889 Browning attended a dinner party at the home of his friend, the artist Rudolf Lehmann. The highlight of which was a recording made on a wax cylinder on an Edison cylinder phonograph. On the recording, which still exists, Browning recites part of How They Brought the Good News from Ghent to Aix, and can even be heard apologising when he forgets the words.

The recording was first played in 1890 on the anniversary of his death, at a gathering of his admirers, it was said to be the first time anyone's voice 'had been heard from beyond the grave'.

His last work Asolando: Fancies and Facts (1889), returned to his brief and concise lyric verse that was so popular. It was published on the day of his death on December 12th, 1889, Robert Browning was at his son's home Ca' Rezzonico in Venice.

He was buried in Poets' Corner in Westminster Abbey; his grave lies immediately adjacent to that of Alfred Tennyson.

Among the many who have publicly acknowledged their literary debt to him are Henry James, Oscar Wilde, George Bernard Shaw, G. K. Chesterton, Ezra Pound, Jorge Luis Borges, and Vladimir Nabokov.

Robert Browning - A Concise Bibliography

Here follows a list of the plays and poetry volumes published during his lifetime. Poems of particular worth are noted from within those volumes.

Pauline: A Fragment of a Confession (1833)
Paracelsus (1835)
Strafford (play) (1837)
Sordello (1840)
Bells and Pomegranates No. I: Pippa Passes (play) (1841)
     The Year's at the Spring
Bells and Pomegranates No. II: King Victor and King Charles (play) (1842)
Bells and Pomegranates No. III: Dramatic Lyrics (1842)
     Porphyria's Lover
     Soliloquy of the Spanish Cloister
     My Last Duchess
     The Pied Piper of Hamelin
     Count Gismond
     Johannes Agricola in Meditation
Bells and Pomegranates No. IV: The Return of the Druses (play) (1843)
Bells and Pomegranates No. V: A Blot in the 'Scutcheon (play) (1843)
Bells and Pomegranates No. VI: Colombe's Birthday (play) (1844)
Bells and Pomegranates No. VII: Dramatic Romances and Lyrics (1845)
     The Laboratory
     How They Brought the Good News from Ghent to Aix
     The Bishop Orders His Tomb at Saint Praxed's Church
     The Lost Leader
     Home Thoughts from Abroad
     Meeting at Night
Bells and Pomegranates No. VIII: Luria and A Soul's Tragedy (plays) (1846)
Christmas-Eve and Easter-Day (1850)
An Essay on Percy Bysshe Shelley (essay) (1852)
Two Poems (1854)
Men and Women (1855)
     Love Among the Ruins
     A Toccata of Galuppi's
     Childe Roland to the Dark Tower Came
     Fra Lippo Lippi
     Andrea Del Sarto
     The Patriot

www.ingramcontent.com/pod-product-compliance
Lightning Source LLC
Chambersburg PA
CBHW060050050426
42448CB00011B/2380